HOW'S YOUR SOUL?

WHY EVERYTHING THAT MATTERS STARTS WITH THE INSIDE YOU

STUDY GUIDE

SIX SESSIONS

JUDAH SMITH

WITH JUSTIN JACQUITH

NELSON
BOOKS

An Imprint of Thomas Nelson

Published in Nashville, Tennessee, by Nelson Books, an imprint of Thomas Nelson. Nelson Books and Thomas Nelson are registered trademarks of HarperCollins Christian Publishing, Inc.

Unless otherwise indicated, all Scripture quotations are taken from the *English Standard Version*, copyright © 2001, trademarked by Good News Publishers.

Scripture marked MSG taken from *The Message*. Copyright © by Eugene H. Peterson 1993, 1994, 1995, 1996, 2000, 2001, 2002. Used by permission of Tyndale House Publishers, Inc.

Scripture quotations marked NLT are taken from the *Holy Bible*, *New Living Translation*, copyright © 1996, 2004, 2007 by Tyndale House Foundation. Used by permission of Tyndale House Publishers, Inc., Carol Stream, Illinois 60188. All rights reserved.

Thomas Nelson titles may be purchased in bulk for educational, business, fund-raising, or sales promotional use. For information, please e-mail SpecialMarkets@ThomasNelson.com.

Published in association with the literary agency of The FEDD Agency, Inc., Post Office Box 341973, Austin, Texas 78734.

ISBN 978-0-310-08386-3

First Printing September 2016 / Printed in the United States of America

CONTENTS

HOW TO USE THIS GUIDE

Welcome to the *How's Your Soul?* small group Bible study! I'm so excited you've decided to embark on this six-week journey. I believe it will have lasting impact on the health of your soul, on your walk with God, and on other key relationships in your life.

If you've already read the *How's Your Soul?* book, you know why this topic means so much to me. For months now, I've been captivated by the importance of a healthy soul. In part, I think it's because I'm getting older, and I want the years I have left to be even better than the years I've lived. To be honest, though, it's also because I've personally experienced an unhealthy soul from time to time—and I don't want to live there.

Chances are, you know what I'm talking about. Life has a way of overwhelming you with good news and bad news, with work and pleasure, with kids and jobs and deadlines and grief and success. Sometimes it feels unrelenting. Sometimes it feels like too much. And as a result, your soul can suffer.

My passion and my prayer is that through this study guide and the accompanying video, you will be able to take an honest look at the state of your soul. That can seem scary at first, but trust me, it's well worth the effort. It's far better to ask the honest questions now than to try to figure out what went wrong after the fact.

We all have parts of our souls that need a bit of work. There is no shame in that. I believe God wants those who follow him to embody true honesty and acceptance in a world where secrets and facades are the norm. He wants us to create environments where we can all find the help we need—where we can grow together through mutual support and encouragement.

I am so grateful for your willingness to follow Jesus and to let him lead your soul. I believe God has incredible things in store as you embrace the journey ahead! The following suggestions will help you get the most out of this small group study guide.

GROUP SIZE

This study is designed for use in a group setting such as a Bible study, Sunday school class, or other small group gathering. Because the goal of the video and guide is to facilitate participation among all the attendees, the ideal group size is between five and fifteen people. If your group is much larger, consider breaking into two or more groups.

MATERIALS NEEDED

Each participant should have his or her own study guide, which includes video teaching questions, small group discussion questions, and personal studies to deepen learning between sessions.

FACILITATION

Each group should have a facilitator who is responsible for starting the video and keeping track of time during discussions and activities. Facilitators may also read questions aloud and monitor discussions, inviting the group to respond and ensuring that everyone has a chance to participate.

PERSONAL STUDY SESSIONS

During the week, you can maximize the impact of the course with the personal studies provided. Each video session includes several short studies with accompanying questions that will help you think about and apply the week's topic to your life. Each of these studies can be completed in about twenty minutes. The studies are personal and devotional in nature, so feel free to utilize them in whatever way works best for you and your schedule. You may wish to read one each day or two or complete the entire week in one sitting.

WHEN IS MY SOUL HOME?

WELCOME

Welcome to the first session of *How's Your Soul?* Our goal in the next six weeks is to explore what it means to have a healthy soul. The apostle John wrote, "Beloved, I pray that all may go well with you and that you may be in good health, as it goes well with your soul" (3 John 2). We are going to explore what it means to be healthy and whole on the inside: our minds, our wills, and our emotions.

Before we begin, it is helpful to define what we mean by the term *soul*. David wrote in Psalm 103:1, "Bless the LORD, O my soul, and all that is within me, bless his holy name!" In this verse, David equates his soul with his inner self: "All that is within me."

Your soul is "all that is within" you. Your soul is not your eye color or your height. It's not your hairline or your waistline (thank God). It's not your name, your education, or your bank account. Your soul is the invisible but incredibly significant part of you that thinks, feels, and decides.

During this first week, we are asking the question, "When is my soul home?" We will look at the origin and creation of the human soul, which gives us a clue about where our souls can truly be at home, at rest, and at ease.

VIDEO TEACHING

The following are a few key thoughts to note as you watch session one of the video. Use the space provided to jot down personal observations or applications.

It is possible to have everything look good on the outside but to be unwell, small, and unsuccessful on the inside. True success is not determined or gauged by the outside but rather by the inside. Much—if not most—of life is the result of who we are on the inside.

When God created Adam, he was just a form. He was just a body. It wasn't until God breathed his own life into him that he became a living soul, a living being. Our outside form isn't what makes us alive—our soul is what makes us alive.

Our souls come from the breath of God. We are living on the borrowed breath of God.

When it comes to our souls, we are often nomadic: our souls don't have a place to belong, a place to rest. They are restless and homeless. But if our physical bodies need a place to call home, how much more do our souls need homes?

God's breath is the origin of our souls. Therefore, our souls return home when we use our borrowed breath to return praise to God.

Psalm 150:6 tells us that everything with breath—everything with a soul—should praise God. Gratitude and worship have incredible power to bring health to our souls.

Mary and Martha illustrate two different approaches to God. Martha was worried and troubled because of what she had to do. She was unwell in her soul. Mary didn't do anything except listen to the love and acceptance of Jesus. Yet Jesus said she had discovered the one essential thing in life.

Our souls find their homes when they return to the creator, God; when they lean into his love, listen to him, and stay close to him. That is when we are truly healthy on the inside.

GROUP DISCUSSION

Take a few minutes to discuss the following questions with your group.

1. How would you define or describe the concept of the soul? What is your soul?

2. How important is it to have a healthy soul? What are some benefits of a healthy soul? What are some negative results of an unhealthy soul?

3. How would you describe the feeling of being at home?

4. What does the idea of our souls needing to go home mean to you?

5. What does the origin of the human soul—when God breathed into Adam's lifeless body and created a living soul—indicate about the soul's original home?

6. What was the difference between Mary's approach to Jesus and Martha's? What do you think the "one thing" was that Mary did?

CLOSING PRAYER

Close your time together in prayer. Here are a few ideas of what you could pray about based on the topic of this session:

- Pray for God to help you evaluate the health of your soul and discover areas that could improve.
- Pray that you would be more aware of God's presence and reality in your life.
- Pray that you could, like Mary, learn to just "be with Jesus" and enjoy his love.

- As a practical way of using your soul to bless God, take a few moments to thank God for who he is and what he has done.

WEEKLY CHALLENGE

Once or twice this week, set aside ten minutes to just be with Jesus, like Mary did. It would be helpful to find a quiet place with no distractions. Maybe put on soft music to help you focus. Then spend time just thinking about who God is, what he has done for you, and how much he loves you. If you want, come prepared next week to share how you felt afterward.

RECOMMENDED READING

Review the introduction and chapter 1 in the book *How's Your Soul?* Use the space provided to write any key points or questions you want to bring to the next group meeting.

Personal Study

Session 1

THAT'S AWKWARD

If it weren't for Chelsea, I'd probably forget one of our kids somewhere at least once a week. It's sad but true. I left our oldest son, Zion, in the car outside a burger place when he was literally three days old. Talk about starting off on the wrong foot.

The problem is that multitasking is not my strong suit, especially when the multiple "tasks" happen to be high-energy, highly mobile humanoids. I tend to lose track of them. That's why in our family, one of my main jobs is to make sure our kids enjoy their childhood, while Chelsea's is to make sure they actually *survive* it. It's sort of an arrangement of necessity.

This arrangement was working well until recently when Chelsea came down with infectious mononucleosis, more affectionately known as mono. Mono is also called the "kissing disease" because it's transmitted by saliva, but Chelsea assured me you could also get it from your kids. Seemed slightly suspicious, but I took her word for it.

One of the main symptoms of mono is extreme fatigue. You might feel great when you wake up, but partway through the day you are so exhausted you can't even stand on your feet.

So for quite a few weeks, Chelsea wasn't able to do all the kid-related things she is so good at (and I am so good at avoiding). That meant I had to gingerly, awkwardly, and amateurishly do some stuff I wasn't used to doing. You know, like laundry. And dishes. And cleaning up the bodily excretions children randomly produce.

Full disclosure: grandparents, friends, nannies, babysitters, and little old ladies who didn't know me but saw me struggling in grocery stores also helped. A lot. But still, let it be known that I went *way* out of my comfort zone there for a while. And I did a fairly good job of it, I might add. I actually found myself getting comfortable with things I would previously have done anything to avoid.

Somehow I sense that most of you are unimpressed. Don't judge me—we all have our weaknesses. Mine just happen to be wimpier than yours.

The point is, we naturally avoid uncomfortable, unfamiliar, or awkward situations. But just because something doesn't come easily for us doesn't mean we should avoid it. Actually, life has a way of dropping us into the most wince-inducing scenarios and then abandoning us, and we usually come out better on the other side.

What does this have to do with our souls? I find that a lot of people get uncomfortable when it comes to evaluating their inner selves. They feel awkward and anxious when faced with authentic introspection. Opening up to themselves or others about what is out of alignment on the inside can sound almost terrifying. So they simply avoid soul-searching at any cost—like me with household chores.

How about you? When was the last time you looked at the state of your soul? How comfortable are you with asking thoughtful, revealing questions about the state of your inner self? That can quickly get nerve-racking, because we aren't used to thinking this way. Usually it's the "outside us"—our health, finances, families, careers—that gets most of our focus. When we do pay attention to the condition of our souls, it's usually because our emotions or thoughts are screaming in desperation.

I'm so angry right now.

I'm scared to death.

I feel betrayed and abandoned.

My life isn't worth living.

But we shouldn't wait until our souls have entered crisis mode before we start listening to them. I believe God wants to give us a level of peace, stability, joy, and hope on the inside that is beyond what we can imagine. He wants to help our souls be at rest no matter what our worlds might look like on the outside.

For that to happen, we have to get comfortable with awkward questions. Questions about our feelings, our thoughts, our fears, our motives, and our needs. Questions that are hard to answer not just because the answers are elusive, but also because the answers are embarrassing. Questions that reveal what is hurting us and hindering us, even if it might take some gut-level courage to deal with what we discover.

The apostle John wrote this to one of his close friends: "Beloved, I pray that all may go well with you and that you may be in good health, as it goes well with your soul" (3 John 2). I believe he was expressing God's heart for each of us: that our souls would be happy, healthy, and whole.

God wants to help us with our soul searching and soul healing more than we might realize. He is committed not just to our happiness—which is notoriously fleeting and subjective—but also to our well-being. And that well-being starts on the inside.

Are you up to the challenge? Are you willing to face the dirty dishes, crumpled laundry, and random bodily fluids of your soul? Okay, I might have just pushed that analogy too far. But you get the point. *Comfort zones are overrated.*

Your soul is you, and you are your soul, and you are definitely worth taking care of. So don't be too afraid, too busy, or even too selfless to start paying attention to your soul. You'll be glad you did.

- Are you comfortable talking with other people about your feelings, hurts, dreams, and desires? If not, why do you think it's difficult for you?

- I'VE GOTTEN BETTER. STILL NOT SOMETHING I JUMP AT

- JUDGEMENT, SEEING THROUGH THE FACADE

- Why do you think people often wait until their souls are in crisis mode before they think about them? Do you tend to do this?

  - IGNORANCE
  -PROCRASTINATION
  - LACK OF RESOURCES
  - NOT SURE WHERE TO GO FOR HELP

- Take a moment to think about the state of the inner you. Then write down at least three specific fears, feelings, assumptions, or insecurities that might be affecting you.

  - SCHEDULE INTERVENTION
  -

STALKER GOD

Have you ever felt like you knew someone just because you followed that individual on social media? You've had zero personal interaction in real life, but you're basically BFFs—at least in your mind. You notice when she gets a new haircut. You feel bad when you see a photo of him with a broken leg. Or you find yourself personally offended when the person makes a bad decision or posts a picture of questionable taste.

Do you remember when observing someone from a distance was considered creepy? That used to be called spying, by the way. Or stalking, or prying, or snooping, or staring. Your mom probably told you not to do it.

Now we call it *following*, because social media and modern technology have turned staring at people into a normal part of life. We even brag about the number of spies/stalkers/snoopers attached to our own social media accounts, because being watched from a distance must mean we are important.

I'm not here to criticize social media. I love it, actually—probably too much. Just ask my wife and kids, who I stalk regularly with my camera phone in hand. Snapchat is my current obsession, but I've gone through a Twitter phase, an Instagram phase, and a Periscope phase. I've never had a LinkedIn phase. That probably says something about me.

Our fixation with following happens to be a good illustration of a couple of realities that can affect how well we know our souls. These aren't new phenomena, by the way—they are as old as humanity itself. Social media just makes the issues more obvious.

Let me explain.

First, when it comes to *others*, we often jump to conclusions without knowing people's hearts. We label them awesome or arrogant, remarkable or ridiculous, clever or clueless. We critique their romantic choices. We pick apart their fashion. Based purely on their online posts, we think we know the contents of people's souls, and we are authorized and obligated to publish a response.

Second, when it comes to *ourselves*, we tend to project a persona we think will be accepted by others. That usually means we focus primarily on the outside. Why? Because we know very well how quick we are to judge superficially, and we fear that other people are doing the same to us.

This fascination with our facades, our exteriors, and

our appearances means that the inside us—which is far more important—often remains unknown. Not only to others, but even to ourselves. We genuinely don't know if we are at peace. We don't know if our minds are in a healthy place. We don't know if our desires and decisions are right.

We like to think we know other people, but do we even know ourselves? Can we sort through the confusing barrage of emotions and thoughts and really judge ourselves?

I don't think we can. At least not completely.

We can and should do our best, of course. But ultimately, only one person knows us completely. He's been watching and following us, not from a distance, but from right next to us.

That person, as I'm sure you've already guessed, is God. God is the creator of every human soul. He sees the inner you. He knows your thoughts and feelings and decisions. He watches your past, present, and future at the same time. If anyone is qualified to make an accurate, comprehensive evaluation about the inside you, it's God.

The prophet Jeremiah wrote this about God's insight:

> *The heart is hopelessly dark and deceitful,*
> *a puzzle that no one can figure out.*
> *But I, God, search the heart*
> *and examine the mind.*
> *I get to the heart of the human.*
> *I get to the root of things.*
> *I treat them as they really are,*
> *not as they pretend to be.*
> (Jeremiah 17:9–10 MSG)

How does that passage make you feel? If you're like me, you might feel a bit nervous. I'm not too proud of some things deep within me. There are a few recesses in my soul that I'm trying to ignore. The idea that God is searching and examining the inner me can make me uncomfortable.

But in reality, this shouldn't be threatening—it should be comforting. God isn't watching us to criticize us, shame us, or judge us. He wants to help us.

Yes, our insides might be a bit embarrassing at times, but God isn't turned off by that. He knows exactly who we are, and he loves us anyway. He has loved us since before we even thought about him. He loves us when we don't love ourselves. And he will love us forever, regardless of whether we earn or deserve or reciprocate that love.

God is our most avid follower. He's crazy about us. He's madly in love with us. But unlike social media stalkers, God actually does know us—far better than we know ourselves.

In your journey of finding health on the inside, start by turning to God. He is the only one capable of truly knowing you.

- On a scale of 1 to 10, how well do you think you know yourself? Is it possible to truly know yourself? Why or why not?

- Are there any areas of your life that you are a bit nervous about having God examine? Write a couple of them down. Why does it make you uncomfortable that God might see those things?

- If God is your most avid fan and follower, how do you think he responds when he sees something inside you that needs to improve?

JUST STOPPING BY

Spending time visiting friends and relatives is great. Right? Hanging out at their homes, laughing, eating, and playing card games—I highly recommend it. It's awesome.

Except when it's not.

Maybe you have one or two people in your life whom you don't love visiting. It's not that you don't love them as individuals—it's the environment they live in that is hard to handle. It's the house. It's the odor. It's the toilet bowl that hasn't been cleaned since 1986. It's the pet that ambushes you at the door with way too much affection and hair.

You love them, but you just prefer to love them from a distance. Or at least from a neutral location. But Christmas comes around, and you find yourself standing on the doorstep again.

You know you are visiting one of these people when this telltale phrase slips out of your mouth as soon as you walk in the door: "We're just stopping by."

Have you ever said that? The door creaks open. You smell the smells and see the sights. You look sideways at your spouse, and your spouse looks back. In unspoken agreement you say, "Aunt Ruthie, hi! Wow, we love you. And . . . your five cats! Um, we can't stay long. *We're just stopping by.*" You don't pre-plan to say it. You assess the situation, and it springs out of the deep places of your heart. "Cousin Frank, so great to see you! Hey, we are just stopping by!"

As soon as politely possible, you make your exit and head home. To *your* home. When you walk in your own door, you are flooded with a completely different emotion and sensation. It's familiar, comforting, reassuring. You are finally home.

Even if your house is small, even if you are renting, even if the neighbors play their music too loud, even if it's not a house at all, just a room or a shared apartment—it's still *home*. It's still yours. If you find a hair on the bathroom counter, you know who it belongs to. If you see a dirty dish lying around, at least the germs are in the family.

There's nothing quite like the feeling of coming home, and there's nothing quite like other people's homes to make you value your own. So ask yourself: *If your physical self needs a home so much, how much more does your soul need a home?*

The truth is, many people never find a home for their souls. They never find a haven, a safe place, a refuge where their inner selves can kick off their shoes and completely relax. They spend their lives making sure their external selves have a place to live, food to eat, and other necessities, but they neglect their souls— which are far more important.

I think if most of us were to slow down for a moment, we'd realize that often our souls are longing for home. Some of us have gotten so used to visiting uncomfortable places on a soul level that we don't even know what home feels like. Instead of just stopping by, we've moved in. We've taken up residence in homes called doubt, insecurity, anxiety, and frustration.

God wants to help your soul find its way home. He wants you to feel as comfortable on the inside as you feel on the outside when you walk into that familiar, welcoming place you call home.

The big question is, when are our souls home? It's easy to agree that our souls need to find that place of rest, of refuge, of relaxing. But where exactly is it?

The answer isn't complicated, but isn't the most obvious, either. We are used to assuming that peace on the inside is the result of peace on the outside. So we work hard to try to eliminate danger, hurt, and risk so that our souls can finally feel at home and at rest.

But the ultimate home of the soul is not found in this life, because the soul is eternal. The soul is the creation and the reflection of God himself, and it naturally longs for something beyond the confines of this planet. It longs for God.

God created the soul, and the soul is home when it returns to God.

The book of Genesis describes the creation of the human soul this way: "GOD formed Man out of dirt from the ground and blew into his nostrils the breath of life. The Man came alive—a living soul!" (2:7 MSG).

In other words, God started this whole thing called life. And life began not when he made our physical bodies but when he made our *souls*. His breath gave us life. We are living on borrowed breath, you could say, so it's only natural that our souls long to return to their original source and home.

The world around us, exciting as it is, is not really home for our souls. We are just stopping by. We can't stay long, because nothing in this world can ultimately satiate and satisfy the longings of our inner beings.

If you find within yourself a yearning for something that life can't seem to give you, it might be your soul catching your eye and telling you it's time to move on from petty pursuits. It might be God himself calling to the inside you, inviting you to return home.

Maybe you feel far from God. Let me encourage you that the journey home is not difficult, long, or perilous. It doesn't require massive self-control or impossible self-sacrifice. It simply requires faith, which is nothing more than an openhanded, childlike acceptance of Jesus' love and forgiveness.

Maybe you have followed Jesus for years, but the cares and concerns of life have gotten in the way of your relationship with him, and your soul hasn't been home in a long time. You used to love God and life, but something seems to have changed. You find yourself worn and weary, wondering where all the wonderment went. God invites you to return to him, to rest in him.

No matter where you are in life, you can simply open your heart to God and allow your soul to reconnect to him. In God, your soul is home.

- Why do you think we often neglect the state of our souls? Is this an issue for you? Why or why not?

- What does the phrase, "the soul is home when it returns to God," mean to you?

- When was the last time you felt that your soul was truly home, and you felt genuine peace, rest, and belonging on the inside?

Session 2

WHAT MAKES MY SOUL HEALTHY?

WELCOME

Welcome to the second session of *How's Your Soul?*, as we continue our discussion about how to be healthy, happy, and successful on the inside.

Last week, we saw that our souls need a home. *Home* simply means returning to God, the creator of the human soul. Our souls are able to rest and feel at home when they are close to God. This week, we will explore the question, "What makes my soul healthy?" and look at practical ways we can invest in the health of our souls.

When God created Adam and Eve, he placed them in an optimal environment. It was the perfect setting for the human soul to thrive. As we look at the original context of the human soul, we see four God-given elements of a healthy soul environment: rest, restriction, responsibility, and relationship. Together let's take a look at these four elements in a bit more detail.

VIDEO TEACHING

The following are a few key thoughts to note as you watch session two of the video. Use the space provided to jot down personal observations or applications.

Cultivating a healthy soul can seem like a daunting task. What steps should we take? What is good for our souls? The answer is found in Scripture. God has given us a blueprint to live healthy, successful lives on the inside.

Genesis 2 describes the original environment God created for the human soul. Here we see the context in which the soul can thrive.

When sin entered the human race, it became the most detrimental, destructive, and dominant issue. That is why Jesus came to earth. Now that our sin is covered through Jesus, we can go back to the original creation account and discover the elements that are healthy for our souls.

The Garden of Eden was a beautiful, flawless, sinless utopia. It was pleasing to the senses and restful to the soul. This illustrates the first element of a healthy soul environment: *rest*.

In the Garden of Eden, Adam and Eve could eat from all the trees except one. Besides showing us how gracious God is, this also shows us the second element of a healthy soul environment: *restriction*. The word *no* is one of the most powerful words for the human soul.

God gave Adam a job: to tend and keep the garden. This shows us the third element of a healthy soul environment: *responsibility*. Work is a gift from God. God wants us to enjoy our labor and our jobs.

The most important element of a healthy soul environment is seen in God's creation of Eve: *relationship*. God said it was not good for man to be alone, so he was intentional about giving Adam the perfect companion. This is a picture not just of marriage but also of the importance of friendship and companionship.

GROUP DISCUSSION

Take a few minutes to discuss the following questions with your group.

1. Is it hard for you to slow down and enjoy life? Why or why not?

2. What benefits do you find when you get enough rest?

3. Have you noticed how restrictions and limits actually help your soul? What are some examples of a "good no," or areas of life where restrictions are necessary and healthy?

4. Why do you think work tends to have such a bad connotation in our culture?

5. Describe some times when you saw firsthand how work and responsibility were good for your soul.

6. Are you intentional about your friendships? What benefits have you experienced personally from the relationships in your life?

CLOSING PRAYER

Close your time together in prayer. Here are a few ideas of what you could pray about based on the topic of this session:

- Pray for wisdom to know how to cultivate a healthy soul.
- Pray for the ability to truly rest.
- Pray that you would recognize and flourish within healthy limits and restrictions.
- Pray for grace to discover and enjoy your God-given responsibilities.
- Pray for healthy relationships in every area of life, including marriage, family, friends, school, and career.

WEEKLY CHALLENGE

Rest: Take a minute to evaluate your sleep patterns and your stress level. What is one practical thing you could do this week to help you truly rest?

Restriction: What is one thing you could decide to say no to this week that isn't necessarily wrong or bad but is not healthy for your soul?

Responsibility: Write down the top two things you dislike about your job (or responsibilities, if you aren't employed). Then decide if you need to (a) change jobs, (b) change something specific about your job, or (c) change your attitude. Which did you pick?

Relationship: Who are the people with the most influence in your life? Is there someone specific you should add to your circle of friends who is good for your soul? Is there someone who is influencing you that you need to limit because he or she is actually harming your soul?

RECOMMENDED READING

Review chapter 2 in the book *How's Your Soul?* Use the space provided to write any key points or questions you want to bring to the next group meeting.

Personal Study

YOU NEED GOLF

My dad was not just a golfer: he was a golf *evangelist*. His goal in life was to get as many people golfing as possible. He might not have been the greatest golfer in the world, but he had more passion and love and sheer joy for the sport than just about anyone I've met.

I also love golf, but I'm not as good as my dad about dragging newbies along with me. I think that's because I'm a bit competitive. And by "a bit" I mean way too much. Just ask my longsuffering golfing buddies or look at the dents in my golf clubs. They all tell the same story. So I tend to golf with people who I can either barely beat or people who won't get offended if I throw my clubs when they beat me. That's a relatively narrow demographic.

My dad, though, would golf with anyone. I lost track of how many people he convinced to take up golf. If he found out you were the least bit interested, he wouldn't just invite you to play with him. He'd pay for your game, buy you a couple boxes of balls and a shirt, and sooner or later buy you a set of clubs.

He was an expert at overcoming excuses people made when he tried to convert them into golfers. My favorite was when people would say, "I would golf, but I just don't have time for it. It's like a five-hour game! If golf were nine holes instead of eighteen, then maybe I'd play. But it just takes too long."

And my dad would say, "Well, that's the point."

"What do you mean?"

"You're too busy *not* to golf. If you can't spare half a day to wander God's green hills, breathe fresh air, enjoy breathtaking views, and rejuvenate yourself in the sunshine and smells and sounds of nature, then your schedule has a problem. If you don't have time for golf, that just proves how much you need golf."

It was an airtight argument, and he probably had more golfer converts than most professional golfers. Of course, he neglected to mention that golfing in Seattle often involves more rain than sunshine. Or that you spend more time in God's green weeds looking for lost balls than wandering those green hills. Or that trying to hit a little white ball consistently can be more frustrating and stressful than running a million-dollar company. But he knew that by the time they figured that out, they'd be hooked, and it would be too late.

The older I get, the more I appreciate Dad's point. Our souls need regular rest. They need breaks. They need moments when they can disconnect from the craziness of life and just enjoy the moments they are in.

Maybe golf isn't relaxing to you. I'm not going to try to change your mind. As I said, I'm not the evangelist my dad was. But if you want a healthy soul, you do need to figure out how to find authentic rest for your soul on a regular basis.

The book of Psalms says this:

> *It is in vain that you rise up early*
> *and go late to rest,*
> *eating the bread of anxious toil;*
> *for he gives to his beloved sleep.*
> (Psalm 127:2)

This passage is so practical that we usually over-spiritualize it. I'll get to the spiritual application in a minute, but honestly, the psalmist here is talking about *literal* sleep. He is talking about hitting the pillow (or whatever they used back then) and instantly sinking into satisfying slumber. Forget counting sheep. That was his day job. Night was for rest.

Sometimes we don't rest well because we are worried about our daily responsibilities. Somehow we think that if we stay awake a bit longer—if we set the alarm a little earlier—we'll be able to solve all of tomorrow's troubles. But often we end up stealing rest not just from our bodies but also from our souls. And in the long run, that is the most counterproductive thing we can do.

Don't misunderstand me. Hard work is a part of life. I'm not against work, exertion, or even exhaustion. There are seasons and moments when we will put in long, hard hours, and our sleep may suffer. But that can't be our lifestyle 24–7, week after week. We need a habit of rest. We need a philosophy and an outlook on life that says, "I don't have all the answers, and that's okay. God does. He can do more while I sleep than I can when I'm awake.

So I'm just going to do my best, and I'm going to rest in the fact that God is in control and on my side."

Ultimately, of course, God wants us to have rest in our souls, not just our bodies. But the two are connected. It's harder to be at rest on the inside when you are not resting well on the outside. And it's easier to handle external pressures and problems when your soul is healthy and relaxed.

Rest is not the result of an absence of problems. You won't have that until heaven. So unless you're planning to stay stressed out for your entire life, you need to figure out how to find soul rest even when your life has a measure of stress, risk, and danger.

The true source of rest is Jesus. He told his followers, "Come to me, all of you who are weary and carry heavy burdens, and I will give you rest. Take my yoke upon you. Let me teach you, because I am humble and gentle at heart, and you will find rest for your souls" (Matthew 11:28–29 NLT).

- What do you do to unwind and rest? How often do you do this?

- How does too much stress affect you emotionally? Physically? Spiritually?

- What does it mean to you that Jesus is the source of true rest? How can you find rest for your soul in him?

THE GOOD NO

Recently in the Smith household, we've been working with our kids on what we call "daily routines." Or as my little Gracie calls them, "daywee wootines." I hope she never stops talking like that.

These daily routines are not difficult, by the way. I'm not talking about child labor. I'm talking about brushing teeth, picking up dirty laundry, and straightening the house. These are time-honored tasks that children down through the ages have been responsible for. So it never ceases to surprise me when one of my offspring reacts as if this were a form of child abuse.

"Elliott, it's time to brush your teeth."

"I don't feel like it. Can I do it tomorrow?"

"No, your teeth will turn yellow, and your breath will smell bad. It will take you two minutes. Just do it."

"But Daaaaaaaaad! I can't!"

"The toothbrush and toothpaste are right in front of you. You have two hands. You are conscious. I don't understand the problem here."

"My feet hurt."

"I'm sorry. Luckily you don't need your feet to brush your teeth. Sit on a chair while you brush."

"Nooooooo!"

If you have kids, you can probably relate. For that matter, if you are human, you can probably relate. Maybe you and I don't object to dental hygiene anymore, but as humans we tend to resist commands, impositions, and restrictions. Even though we might understand mentally that they are necessary, there is something about having to submit that often stirs up resistance in our souls.

That's why the Genesis account of creation is fascinating to me. The first two chapters of the Bible describe a gorgeous, perfect, and sin-free environment. This was the original home for the soul. These were the surroundings God created for the soul to thrive. There were trees, lakes, animals, gold, and, of course, sex. In other words, God wanted us to enjoy our lives. He wanted us to rest and relax.

But that's not the whole story. Right in the middle of describing the incredible beauty and pleasure of the Garden of Eden, God mentions a restriction. "You can eat from every tree you see . . . except one. Just one. See this little guy over here? He's off limits. If you eat that fruit, you'll die. So go enjoy the rest of the creation, but don't eat from this tree."

But God, I always think when I read that. *I thought creation was perfect. I thought you said all of it was good. So why would you create something and then tell Adam and Eve they couldn't have it?*

First of all, God was allowing them to *choose* to love him. That's a topic for another time, but let me just state that love needs to be a choice in order for it to be real love. Adam and Eve weren't puppets. They weren't Pinocchios. They had to be able to make a free-will choice, or they wouldn't truly have been able to love.

But I think God was also sending us a message. He was saying that restriction is *good*. That limitations are healthy. That having certain things off limits is actually a necessary requirement for a strong, sane soul. God didn't apologize for that tree. He knew it was good for Adam and Eve to tell themselves *no* from time to time.

The fact there were thousands or maybe millions of trees they *could* eat from, and only one they *couldn't* eat from, says a lot about God. He is not a restrictive God. He is a liberating God—a God who loves to give his children enjoyment, pleasure, opportunity, and freedom.

But just as love is not love without choice, so freedom is not freedom without restrictions. True liberty is found within limits. The optimal environment for the human soul is not just great freedom; it is great freedom exercised within absolute boundaries.

The Corinthian church struggled a bit with this concept. They embraced the freedom they had in Christ, but a teaching began to circulate that true freedom meant no restrictions, no restraints, no rules. They started using this mentality to justify sexual immorality and other destructive lifestyles.

So Paul wrote this: "You say, 'I am allowed to do anything'— but not everything is good for you. And even though 'I am allowed to do anything,' I must not become a slave to anything" (1 Corinthians 6:12 NLT). In other words, just because you *can* doesn't mean you *should*. Just because the tree was there didn't mean Adam and Eve should have eaten from it. Just because we can spend money on something, or participate in some activity, or go to a certain place doesn't mean doing so will be helpful for us.

Our freedom in Jesus is not just to say *yes*; it's also to say *no*. Think about that. The word *no* is one of the most freeing in the English language. In Jesus, we are free to say no to harmful, hurtful, destructive things. We are no longer slaves to our desires or addictions. We are free to live within healthy boundaries.

I am not here to list the things everyone should say no to. Neither are you, by the way. Christians are famous (or infamous) for trying to control other people's consciences, usually with limited success. That's God's job. The Holy Spirit, who is God's presence here on earth with each of us, will help us know what to say yes to and what to say no to.

Rather than viewing restrictions as evil or limiting, begin to view them as healthy for your soul. You are free to live a wholesome, happy life as you embrace the limits God has given.

- How do you tend to respond when you are told no?

- What are some restrictions in your life that might actually be good rather than bad?

- How do you think restrictions and restraints help make our souls healthy?

TGIF

What is your emotional reaction to Mondays? Maybe that's a depressing opening question—especially if today happens to be Monday for you. If so, it just proves my point, as you'll see.

I've never conducted a scientific poll on the topic—and I never will on any topic—but it's my observation that most of us are not big fans of Mondays. As a matter of fact, many people seem to think Monday is the worst day of the week. It's not hard to understand why. After a weekend of rest, relaxation, and revelry, now you have an entire week of school or work ahead of you. You have to get up before you want to; you have responsibilities to attend to; you have things to accomplish. Mondays are so bad the birds don't even sing. Butterflies turn back into caterpillars. Food tastes like it's healthy. You get the point.

Looking at the rest of the week, it seems that Tuesday and Thursday are pretty much nondescript. But Wednesdays are now called "hump day." Have you heard that term?

I had to ask someone what it meant, because it sounded disturbing.

He responded, "It's Wednesday. Every Wednesday is hump day."

I was like, "What are you talking about?"

"You know, Wednesday. It's halfway through the week. Once you get past Wednesday, you are over the hump. You are headed for the weekend. There is hope that you'll live to see Saturday and Sunday." Makes sense.

Then you have Friday. Friday is the complete opposite of Monday. On Friday, you don't even need coffee. Just the mere realization that Friday has arrived is enough to make you smile, sing in the car, and stop for pedestrians. Friday has songs written about it. Friday has restaurants dedicated to it (well, one anyway). Friday is an indelible and delightful part of pop culture, because Friday is the official start of the goal of the whole week: the weekend.

Have you ever stopped to think about what this says about our culture? Our fixation with Friday is a commentary on our attitude toward responsibility. Many times we think that work or school are about what we *have* to do, and evenings and weekends are about what we *want* to do. We put up with the pain, toil, and trouble of this necessary evil so we can party later (or nap, depending on our personality and/or age).

Our culture tends to view retirement the same way. Work hard for forty-plus years so you can relax, play golf, and maybe tour the countryside in an RV. If you ask me, driving and sleeping in an RV sounds like the opposite of relaxing, but to each his own.

I think many of us assume hard work is a curse. It's punishment. We even use the Bible to back up our belief: God told Adam after he sinned, "By the sweat of your face you shall eat bread" (Genesis 3:19). I read that and I'm like, *He's going to eat with a sweaty face? That's kind of graphic, God. Sweat is gross.*

If you look closely at the story of creation—which we have described as the optimal, God-designed environment for the soul—responsibility actually predates sin. Right after the Bible describes the creation of man, it says, "The LORD God took the man and put him in the garden of Eden to work it and keep it" (Genesis 2:15).

Work is not a result of humanity's fall. It isn't a curse. Yes, there is a frustration, a desperation, and a futility often attached to work that wasn't part of God's original design. But work itself is not evil.

God worked, and he worked hard. Actually, he worked for six days—not five—before he took a break. And I don't think he was depressed on Monday, or that he took heart when it was hump day, or that he counted down the days until Friday. He worked when it was time to work, and he enjoyed the results of his work. Then he rested when it was time to rest, and he seems to have enjoyed that, too.

Our souls need responsibilities. We need to work to challenge ourselves, to tackle obstacles, and to produce results. That doesn't mean we should be workaholics, of course. Our identities should not be wrapped up in what we do, nor should we stake our ultimate satisfaction and value in our careers. But our souls will feel better and be healthier when they are fulfilling their God-given capacity to work.

I can't define what *work* will mean for you. I don't know what responsibilities, callings, or giftings you have, or what God has planned for your future. That is between you and him. Even if your current job, occupation, or day-to-day schedule is not what you see yourself doing long-term, it's helpful to remember that responsibility itself is healthy for your soul. You were created to make a difference and to produce results. Don't be surprised if God starts opening doors and you find yourself busy—even overwhelmed at times—with ever greater responsibilities.

As we saw earlier, rest is an essential component of a healthy soul environment. Don't neglect rest. But responsibility is also essential. The two work together, and either one without the other is less than ideal.

I am confident that God will give you the direction and grace you need to follow him and do his work. And as you do, your soul will find itself in a place of ever increasing health.

- What are some of your day-to-day responsibilities?

- How have you seen work affect the health of your soul? Does it help or hurt you? Why?

- How could you facilitate the benefits of responsibility
  for your soul? That is, are there things you could do
  differently so your responsibilities can make your soul
  healthier?

THAT'S MY COFFEE

The coffee culture in the upper left corner of the United States is
getting out of control. Most of us who live here have been assim-
ilated into the system and the philosophy of coffee without even
realizing it.

I haven't always been part of that culture. I didn't even used
to like coffee. My wife slowly convinced me to start drinking it in
the morning. Then one day she asked, "Can you make the coffee
today?" And ever since then, I've either been making it for her or
taking her out to buy it. Is that how addicts do it? You get a friend
to join you, and then you get him to start paying for it?

Coffee has a lingo all its own: ristretto, macchiato, half-caf,
room, extra room—it's standard vocabulary for the Northwest.
And people are emotionally invested in the coffee they order.
Spend five minutes in a coffee shop, and you'll hear the nuances
and variations of popular drinks discussed as if happiness can be
found in the perfect shot.

There is a fair bit of coffee snobbery as well. It typically manifests itself when a coffee newbie is at the front of the line, and she feels compelled to ask the barista what every term on the chalkboard means before picking a drink. You can watch the line become visibly agitated, as if the person should have done more research before entering this sacred place.

I become more aware of this culture every time I visit parts of the United States where people are less addicted to caffeine. We were at a restaurant in Atlanta a while back, and I asked if I could get an Americano. Our server was clearly confused by the term. "Hold on, let me look that up."

I said, "Do you have hot water?"

"Yeah."

"Okay, put two shots of espresso in a cup, add hot water, and kind of swirl it around a bit."

I was nice about it. I certainly didn't try to specify a temperature. You know you are a consummate consumer of coffee if you start throwing around the specific number of degrees to which you want your beverage heated. For the record, I like my coffee at 165 degrees. I don't want 180 degrees, and I don't want 150 degrees. I want that just-right Goldilocks temperature.

The reason I ask for my coffee at a certain temperature is because I don't drink coffee. I gulp it. I can finish my drinks in an inordinately short amount of time.

Normally that's not a problem, but recently Chelsea and I shared a large coffee. It was actually our third latte of the day, which is why we decided to split it. We were shopping, and I was carrying this ridiculously large coffee out in front of me, with my elbow bent at the standard ninety-degree angle. I have no idea why coffee must be carried that way, but we all do it.

Anyway, I was shopping and talking and gulping. Then Chelsea said, "Could I have a sip? I haven't had any of that coffee yet."

Suddenly I became aware that the cup, still at a ninety-degree angle, was feeling really light. I panicked a bit. I shook the cup, and then I peeked inside. There was nothing but cold foam at the bottom. It turns out I had finished the whole thing.

Have you ever split a latte with your spouse? That is the quickest way to end up in marriage counseling. You thought you and your significant other were really close? Try sharing a latte. If you make it through that, you can survive anything.

I am not free to discuss the comments and insinuations and emotional shrapnel that were directed at me upon the discovery that I had finished the entire drink. Safe to say, we no longer share coffee, because experience has shown it is not healthy for our marriage. It's just not worth it.

Our little latte troubles are a silly illustration of an important principle: sharing life with other people can be hard. Involving other people in our goals, dreams, and desires can sometimes feel so complicated that we wonder if it's really worth it.

Maybe I would be better off on my own, we think. *This friendship is too frustrating. My marriage has become too painful. I think I should go solo for a while. Just me, myself, and I. What a team.*

Refusing to share a coffee with someone is one thing, but refusing to share life with other people is another. Yet sometimes we do just that, especially after a particularly painful experience. We think that relationships are optional. We decide that friendships are nice but not essential. We assert to the world around us that we are strong enough and smart enough to make it on our own.

That independence sounds more American than Starbucks, but I can tell you right now it's misguided—and ultimately harmful. God created our souls with a built-in need for relationship. We were not designed to be alone. No matter how strong, independent, or self-reliant we are, we need other people, and other people need us.

In the creation story, time after time God looked at the elements he was making and said, "It is good." There is only one recorded instance where he said something was "not good," and it's found in Genesis 2:18: "It is not good that the man should be alone; I will make him a helper fit for him."

Specifically, of course, God was talking about finding Adam a wife. Marriage is awesome, and I highly recommend it. After all, what other person in my life would forgive me—eventually—for drinking her coffee? That's true love.

In a larger sense, however, I believe this story shows the value God places on family, friendship, and companionship. Just look at how much work he went to in order to give Adam and Eve the perfect relationship. Relationship is a genuine goal and value for God, and he cares about our friendships even more than we do.

I can't even imagine where my life would be without friends and family members who genuinely care for me. And even if you've experienced some painful relational moments, chances are, you agree with me. There are letdowns and hang-ups along the way, but ultimately friendships enrich our lives like nothing else.

Relationships are the only thing worth holding on to. Fame, money, possessions, appearances—they will come and go in this life. But true friends will sustain us and surround us throughout our lives.

Relationships are essential for healthy souls. So let's not do life alone.

- Do you consider yourself a good friend? Why or why not?

- Describe a time when a friend or family member helped you with something significant that you couldn't have accomplished on your own.

- How do good relationships help your soul stay healthy?

WHY DOES MY SOUL HAVE HOPE?

WELCOME

Welcome to the third session of *How's Your Soul?* We are halfway through a six-week journey of self-discovery and God-discovery, looking at how to be healthy and fulfilled on an internal/soul level.

Last week, we looked at four specific elements that contribute to a healthy soul environment: rest, restriction, responsibility, and relationship. This week, we will explore the question, "Why does my soul have hope?"

If you're like me, you've probably experienced moments when your emotions or thoughts seemed to be spiraling out of control, when you were surprised and confused by the turmoil your soul felt. In moments like that, how do we discover—or rediscover—hope? Where can our souls turn in times of trouble? Let's find out.

VIDEO TEACHING

The following are a few key thoughts to note as you watch session three of the video. Use the space provided to jot down personal observations or applications.

Have you ever been shocked by your soul or surprised by your feelings? That's not necessarily a bad thing. The writer of Psalms 42–43 addresses this very topic.

How do we find stability and sanity and clarity in life? This artist addresses his own soul and says, "Hope in God" (Psalm 42:5). God is the only sure source of hope and stability for our souls.

When emotions run high, we need to be intentional about directing our souls to hope in God.

There are only two real options when we are going through hard times: either conclude there is no God and life is meaningless, or believe there is a God and our lives are the result of his plan. If God put us here, then he is God enough to know about and care about our everyday lives.

Even when our souls are in upheaval, God is still in control, and he has a plan and purpose for our lives.

God is a personal God: he is "my salvation and my God" (Psalm 42:5–6). His face is toward us; he is paying attention to our needs. That gives our souls hope.

God is greater than our feelings. He is greater than our souls. That means even when we feel discouraged or condemned, we can hope in him. He loves us, and he cares for us no matter what we are going through.

GROUP DISCUSSION

Take a few minutes to discuss the following questions with your group.

1. Describe a time when your soul felt hopeless or overwhelmed. What did you do to get out of that emotional place?

2. Are the emotional ups and downs of the human experience a bad thing? Why is it important to evaluate your thoughts and emotions in the light of God's love and faithfulness?

3. On a practical level, how can you direct your soul to "hope in God"? What does that mean to you?

4. How does knowing that God is aware of your needs and that he cares for you help you navigate the turmoil your soul sometimes faces?

5. Do you ever have trouble believing God cares for you? Why or why not?

6. What does 1 John 3:20 mean to you: "whenever our heart condemns us, God is greater than our heart, and he knows everything"?

CLOSING PRAYER

Close your time together in prayer. Here are a few ideas of what you could pray about based on the topic of this session:

- Pray for the ability to find hope in God even when your thoughts and emotions are off balance.
- Pray for wisdom to sort through your feelings and be able to trust God.
- Thank God for his eternal, unfailing concern and love toward you. Remember his faithfulness even when things feel out of control.
- Pray that the reality of God's love would supersede emotional conflicts. Pray that you would know and believe how much God cares for you.

WEEKLY CHALLENGE

How do you tend to react when you face strong internal turmoil? Take a moment to think about it, and then write your answer(s) at the top of the next page. You might say things like *escape* (such as through sleep, alcohol, vacation, or hobbies), *be in denial, panic, be indecisive,* or *try to control my environment.* It's important to note that many of those things aren't necessarily wrong; however, they might indicate your soul is looking for hope in the wrong places.

When my soul is overwhelmed, I tend to:

_____

This week, pay special attention to your reactions when your soul starts to feel overwhelmed. Instead of automatically responding, be intentional about placing your hope in God. That could mean taking a moment or two each day to remind yourself God loves you, knows what you are going through, and has a plan for you. If you feel comfortable doing so, come to next week's group prepared to share how hoping in God changed how you reacted in difficult moments.

RECOMMENDED READING

Review chapter 3 in the book *How's Your Soul?* Use the space provided to write any key points or questions you want to bring to the next group meeting.

Personal Study

THE PROBLEM WITH HOPE

I have an inner aversion to birthday parties. I know that sounds depressing, but it's true. It might be due in part to my age. As the years speed by, I am less and less interested in even acknowledging, much less celebrating, another birthday. It might also have to do with the fact that I can't eat dairy or gluten, so birthday cakes just mock me from a distance.

One of my biggest problems with birthdays is the inevitable ceremony of Blowing Out the Birthday Candles. I know this is a treasured, time-honored tradition, but honestly, it's gross. In all the meal-related moments in our lives and cultures, there is no other setting where we encourage another person to blow on our food. I don't go to a steakhouse and tell the waiter, "I'd like my steak medium well. And could you exhale on it, please? Medium well with a dash of saliva."

Yet this is an essential element of birthday parties. There is something fundamentally wrong with that.

It gets worse. I have watched grown adults eating from cakes that their four-year-old blew on. Think about that. If you've ever seen a small child blow out candles, you know it's not just air that is wafting across that pastry.

I've had kids for twelve years, and I have never partaken of any dessert that my children have blown on. Not once. Blow on your own dessert all you want, kids, but leave mine alone. I can't handle the germs.

There is another tradition associated with birthday parties and birthday cakes that is less revolting but just as confusing as blowing out candles: making wishes. Again, who made this up? Have we really thought this through?

On every childhood birthday, even when I was like eighteen years old, my mom would ask right after I blew out the candles and sprinkled the cake, "Judah, did you make a wish?"

I would think, *Mom, I thought we believe in Jesus. You're sending mixed signals here.*

I remember my thirteenth birthday. I was in seventh grade, and Chelsea was at my party. We've known each other our whole lives. I blew out the candles, and sure enough Mom leaned over and asked, "Did you make a wish, buddy?"

I did make a wish. I wished that Chelsea would kiss me. I didn't tell Mom that, though. All I said was, "Yes, Mom."

I was wishing and wanting and hoping for a kiss from my crush. It didn't happen. Well, it did, actually—when I was twenty-one and we were married, she definitely kissed me, and more besides. But at that particular party, I was hoping for a kiss more like in my seventh-grade year.

That brings me to my point. I have never met a person who cites the power of a birthday wish as the reason their dreams came true. No one has ever told me, "I'm twenty-nine years old, and for twenty-nine years I've been blowing out candles and making wishes and eating cake, and all my dreams have come to pass. I am happy, successful, and fulfilled because of birthday wishes."

If we aren't careful, though, we can end up treating the all-important element of hope a bit like birthday wishes. Here's what I mean.

We all believe in hope. We talk about hope; we value hope; we promote hope. We shake our heads at people's sad stories and encourage them not to lose hope. There's nothing wrong with that—the church should be a beacon of hope, and of all people, Jesus followers should be preachers of hope.

But let's be honest. What good does it do for you to tell me to hope? "Hope for the best," you say. And I might reply, "How is hope going to help? Why is hope any better or more effective than a birthday wish?"

In and of itself, hope can't conquer discouragement. Hope has no inherent power to change our circumstances. Since when has hope done anything? Has hope ever grown arms and legs and saved us? Hope has no mystical powers. Why does hope deserve our hope?

We live in a society that proposes we all stay positive and hope for the best. I don't have a problem with that—being a generally positive person is great. I'd much rather hang around a positive person than a negative person. And I've heard research and theories that imply positive thinking and speaking can directly improve our lives, for a variety of reasons. But positivity, hope, and birthday wishes are not the answer. These things ultimately fall short, because hope in hope is no hope at all.

Hope is essential for the human soul, but we must make sure our hope is based on something greater than wishful thinking. Hope is only as powerful as that to which it is connected. That is what makes our hope in Jesus such a safe, secure place for our souls. The writer to the Hebrews says this about our hope:

> We who have fled to him for refuge can have great confidence as we hold to the hope that lies before us. This hope is a strong and trustworthy anchor for our souls. It leads us through the curtain into God's inner sanctuary. Jesus has already gone in there for us.
>
> (Hebrews 6:18–20 NLT)

As Jesus followers, our hope is unique among all other hopes on the planet. It is not attached to our emotions, plans, relationships, or finances, but to Jesus.

Jesus opened the way for us to be united to God. Jesus gives us confidence that we have been forgiven and accepted by God. Jesus is proof that God loves us and is on our side. Jesus is our guarantee of the future.

When our souls lose hope, we have a sure, steadfast, immovable anchor who we can turn to. His name is Jesus, and our hope in him is never misplaced.

- What are some things you've wished for that haven't come true?

- Have you ever felt hopeless? How does that affect your soul, especially if you are without hope for an extended period of time?

- Why is Jesus the best source of hope for our souls?

ARE YOU LISTENING?

I am a very "in the moment" kind of person. I am intensely present. Whatever I am doing at the moment, I am convinced it's the most important, exhilarating thing in the world, and everyone else should be doing it too.

The side effect of being in the moment, though, is that I am also easily distracted. You would think it would be the opposite.

You would think if I'm so engrossed in what I'm doing, nothing should be able to break my attention. Unfortunately, that's not how it works. The "moment" I am so "present" in can and will change without warning.

For example, if you and I are talking, you will have my full and undivided attention. I will be intently, profoundly, genuinely present. Until a refrigerator fan kicks on in the room, or I notice a guacamole stain on your shirt, or a fly sputters into my peripheral vision. And then that new thing will have my full and undivided attention, and I will completely forget whatever you and I were talking about.

That can have negative consequences on relationships, as you can imagine. Especially relationships of the marital variety.

I can be talking excitedly to Chelsea about whatever has most recently captured my imagination, and she listens, because she's an amazing listener. Then she starts to comment. She's insightful and balanced and intelligent, and honestly, I always have every intention of listening to her reply.

Then my phone buzzes, and I look down. I don't think about it. I don't consciously decide to move on to another moment. I just want to make sure no one is trying to reach me urgently, or a sports team hasn't traded a player I need to know about. Important things.

And just like that, she's lost me.

She knows when this happens, of course. Before I do. Subconsciously, I still think I'm listening to her. She has no problem whatsoever calling me out. "Judah, you aren't listening!"

"Hmm? Yes I am, babe."

"You're looking at your phone."

"What?"

"Exactly."

"No, no, sorry, I'm listening. I really want to hear what you have to say. What were we talking about?"

"I scheduled a vasectomy appointment for you."

"Uh-huh, that's so good, babe. I totally agr—*wait, what did you just say*?!"

It's come to the point that my wife has literally started locking my phone in the hotel safe whenever we are on vacation. It is for my own good, she tells me. Otherwise, either my phone or I are going to end up at the bottom of the ocean.

I'm trying to improve, but it's tough when you're such a present, engaged, vivacious person, you know? Is it my fault that I want to enjoy every moment, even if the moment I'm focusing on changes with frightening frequency?

Anyway, if you and I ever meet, I will be delighted to see you. I really will. But if halfway through our conversation my eyes glaze over, don't be hurt. It's not you, as they say—it's me. And if you text me and I don't respond, don't take it personally. I ignore closer friends than you all the time. Chances are, my phone is locked in a hotel safe anyway.

Here's my point: one of the greatest gifts we can give another person is our attention. Why? Because attention implies care and concern. It implies we are there for that person. On the other hand, a lack of attention says we don't care about him or her, and we can't be counted on to help in time of need. That's the message I inadvertently send when my NFL app interrupts my conversations and I mentally check out.

Have you ever felt like God has checked out? Like he is distracted or indifferent or unaware of what you are going through? I know I have.

For our souls to be healthy, they need hope. Hopelessness signals a sick soul, a weak soul, a discouraged soul. We naturally look for reasons to have hope—things like friends, bank accounts, business strategies, and governments. But ultimately, we need a source of hope that is bigger than us. So we turn to God.

If you've been following Jesus for any length of time, though, you have probably run into situations where it seemed God either wasn't aware or didn't care about your pain. When things are going smoothly, it's easy to believe God cares. But when you take one hard hit after another, it can be tough to believe God is paying attention. And if he isn't there for you, you think, then all hope is lost.

The book of Psalms is extraordinarily helpful in these difficult times, because it is a collection of real songs written by real people who were experiencing real troubles. And they aren't shy about their feelings, either.

A common theme runs throughout the emotional carnage on display in this heartfelt book: God is listening, and he cares. Again and again these ancient songwriters remind us God isn't just big, powerful, and holy: he is also paying attention. His face is turned toward us, and he is concerned about what we are going through.

King David wrote this about God:

> *He has never let you down,*
> *never looked the other way*
> *when you were being kicked around.*

He has never wandered off to do his own thing;
he has been right there, listening.
(Psalm 22:24 MSG)

That is incredible. The most powerful being in the universe—scratch that—the *creator* of the universe is watching over us. He is paying attention, he is listening, and he is involved.

Sometimes when my kids were younger, I would be watching TV, and they would want to talk to me. They would climb into my lap, grab my cheeks, and physically turn my head toward them. There was something about knowing I was looking at them that brought them comfort.

Psalms shows there is an infinite, eternal, all-powerful God who cares about your ordinary life. He feels your emotions and hurts. He believes in your dreams and goals. And that gives hope to your soul even in the most difficult times.

- Have you ever felt like God wasn't concerned about what you were going through? Describe your emotions and thoughts during that time.

- Why do you think it is so easy for us to assume God isn't there or doesn't care?

- How does the knowledge that God is paying attention to you and that he cares about you help bring health to your soul?

SURPRISED BY MY SOUL

I might overreact too much.

I say *might* because I don't *feel* like I overreact. In my mind, my reactions are completely justified. Always. The pain, the agony, and the angst I am currently experiencing are real. At least to me.

But I've noticed an alarming trend in the individuals closest to me. I'm talking about my own flesh and blood, those nearest and dearest to me. These are the people who should care the most when I'm in pain—but they are starting to act a little numb.

Recently I was in our kitchen, and I reached up to get a glass from the cupboard. Without warning, searing pain shot through my lower back. I'm talking about debilitating pain. Deep agony. So, naturally, I fell to the kitchen floor and started to moan.

Now, before you criticize me, I had thrown my back out before, and it was one of the most miserably memorable experiences of my life. It took me weeks to recover. Apparently that scarred me on some deep emotional level.

So the instant the spasm hit, I knew my back was out again. I crumpled to the floor and lay there in a fetal position, pathetically rocking back and forth a little, moaning just enough so people would know this was serious but I was brave and could hold myself together.

Chelsea looked over. "You okay?"

"No," I whispered like some sort of martyr. "I just threw my back out. It's bad, babe."

I expected her to rush to my side. To show authentic sympathy. To tell me to hold on, that I'd be okay. Maybe to call an ambulance.

Instead she walked casually to the cupboard and grabbed some Advil.

Advil? I was thinking. *Gee thanks, babe. I need narcotics. I need surgery. I might need a casket.*

Then my kids walked in. More precisely, my kids walked *by*. They might have graced me with a glance, but that was it. They didn't stop. They didn't rush to my side. They didn't ask why Dad was on the kitchen floor writhing and gasping in mortal agony.

My life was flashing before my eyes. I was wondering who would care for our kids if I was paralyzed forever. And how did my family react? Sheer indifference.

Eventually, lying on the floor got uncomfortable. I decided to attempt to stand. I figured I could at lease hobble to the couch and suffer in solitude. I took a few moments to prepare myself mentally for the inevitable pain. Slowly, gingerly, fearfully, I shifted my weight to my knees. I grasped the countertop and pulled myself up.

That's when I discovered I was completely healthy. No pain

or paralysis. I had lain on the floor moaning for ten minutes over a passing muscle spasm—nothing more.

Maybe, possibly, perchance, I tend to overreact.

Have you ever been there? I don't mean on the kitchen floor—I mean have you ever found yourself paralyzed by pain and fear that weren't real? Have you ever discovered that your emotions and your reactions were exaggerated? Have you ever been surprised by your soul?

The songwriter of Psalms 42 and 43 seems to find himself in a similar situation. On one hand, he knows that God is real, powerful, and present. But on the other hand, he feels discouraged and overwhelmed.

As you read through these two psalms, you can see the writer wrestle with his feelings. You can listen as he sorts through the contradictory circumstances and conflicting emotions surging in his soul.

I love the refrain that he pens three times in this passage:

> *Why are you cast down, O my soul,*
> *and why are you in turmoil within me?*
> *Hope in God; for I shall again praise him,*
> *my salvation and my God.*
> (Psalm 42:5–6; see also 42:11; 43:5)

In other words, the psalmist is declaring to his own soul and anyone else who is listening that his hope is in God. His emotions might be going crazy. His soul might be overwhelmed and overcome. He might not be able to wrap his mind around what he's going through. But deep inside, he knows his soul can hope in God.

I love the fact that Psalms validates my tendency to overreact. All right, I might be taking that a little far. But God does validate and even celebrate our human propensity to *feel* life, to experience things on a primal, emotional, and at times illogical level. In moments of pain or danger, we might be surprised by our souls— but God isn't. He holds us, guides us, and stabilizes us, even when our reactions are not exactly full of faith.

Sooner or later, we get up off the kitchen floor. We realize things were not as bad as they seemed. I don't mean the risk or difficulty wasn't real—it probably was. But God is bigger, and he is on our side. Our souls do not have to give in to the fear that seeks to paralyze us, because God is a sure and secure source of confidence.

The next time your soul is cast down and your heart is in turmoil, turn to God. Hope in God. Remember he has helped you before, and he will help you again. Your emotions might betray you, but God never will. He is the hope of your soul.

- Have you ever felt overwhelmed by your circumstances? Describe your emotions and reactions.

- As humans, what things do we try to base our hope on, apart from God? Why are those things an insufficient source of hope?

- How does hoping in God help your soul deal with conflicting emotions and circumstances?

Session 4

WHO DOES MY SOUL HOLD ON TO?

WELCOME

Welcome to the fourth session of *How's Your Soul?* During our sessions together, our goal is to understand what it means to have a healthy soul. The human soul can be defined as the "inside you." It includes your mind, will, and emotions. And as we have seen over the past few weeks, the health of your soul is incredibly significant to the overall quality of your life.

Last week, we talked about how to find hope when our souls feel overwhelmed. We looked at the emotional ups and downs of life and discussed how God is our source of hope even when our feelings betray us.

This week, we will answer the question, "Who does my soul hold on to?" Maybe you've had an experience where you realized you weren't strong enough or smart enough to make it through alone. In moments like those, you become instantly aware that you need a source of stability and strength that is greater than yourself.

VIDEO TEACHING

The following are a few key thoughts to note as you watch session four of the video. Use the space provided to jot down personal observations or applications.

Life is fragile, and challenging moments appear without warning. We need a stable, solid source of confidence and peace.

What Jesus did on the cross for humanity is the ultimate stabilizing, anchoring force for our souls.

Jesus doesn't always make storms disappear immediately, but he is with us in the storm, and he sees us through the storm.

Our souls need outside help. We need a superhero and a savior. But that source of help can't be something without a soul; nor can it be someone who has a soul but has the same struggles we do. Only Jesus qualifies to be the anchor for our souls.

It's not about how tight we hold to the anchor; rather, it's about the anchor who is holding on to us. Our confidence is not in our ability to follow Jesus but in his faithfulness and power to rescue us.

Jesus will not let us go. He is the rock who is higher than us. He is our connection to God. The only sure thing in life is God's grip on us.

When we feel overwhelmed, God nudges us toward himself. He reminds us that he is with us, he loves us, and he will see us through.

GROUP DISCUSSION

Take a few minutes to discuss the following questions with your group.

1. Have you ever found yourself in the middle of unexpected turbulence or danger in life? How did you react?

2. What did Jesus accomplish for us that we can't do for ourselves? How does that function as an anchor for our souls?

3. Why do you think God allows storms in our lives? What should our reaction be in those storms?

4. Why are things or other people insufficient anchors for our soul?

5. Do you ever feel as if you are too weak to hold on to your faith? In those moments, who is holding whom? Are you holding on to God, or is he holding on to you?

6. How does the knowledge that God will never let you go help you face the storms and turbulence of life?

CLOSING PRAYER

Close your time together in prayer. Here are a few ideas of what you could pray about based on the topic of this session:

- Pray for continued trust in Jesus' finished work on the cross. Thank God for his gifts of salvation, strength, and stability through Jesus.
- Pray for God's strength and for an awareness of his presence during times of turbulence or storm.
- Pray that God will help you trust his hold on your life even more than your hold on him.

WEEKLY CHALLENGE

Take a few minutes this week to read the following passages from the book of Psalms. Jot down a few briefs thoughts about each one. These can be personal applications, questions, or observations based on the passage. There is no right or wrong answer: the goal is to interact with the Scripture and let it shape your day-to-day lifestyle.

Psalm 61:2

Psalm 62:5–6

Psalm 91:1–16

RECOMMENDED READING

Review chapters 4 and 6 in the book *How's Your Soul?* Use the space provided to write any key points or questions you want to bring to the next group meeting.

Personal Study

Session 4

PANORAMIC PROBLEMS

I purchased a new iPhone not too long ago. It was an iPhone 6 Plus, which is going to date this writing, because Apple produces a new phone about every twelve minutes. By the time this goes to press, there will probably be an iPhone 13 Extra Mega Plus. It will be the size of a car, and it will make my little 6 Plus look like an antique. Apple always wins.

I discovered my new iPhone has some crazy camera features. I was bragging about them to a friend, and he informed me that my last iPhone had them too. Obviously, I never knew that. Anyway, I now take far too many pictures because I have options like *time-lapse, slo-mo, video, photo, square*, and *pano*.

Remember when you carried actual cameras to family outings? They only had one function: taking pictures. You couldn't download apps or make phone calls on them. They didn't have screens to show you the pictures you had taken. They used actual film, and you didn't need to apply vintage-looking filters because your pictures already looked that way.

You would line up the family and take one picture. That was it—one picture for the day, or maybe two just to be safe. If you really wanted to go all out, you would shoot an entire roll of twenty-four. Nowadays, I take twenty-four pictures of just a pile of leaves. Or well-shaped clouds. Or my own face, because someone invented selfies, and somehow narcissism is now okay.

The other day I had my kids get up on a picnic table bench, and I told them to jump so I could get them in slow motion. After I recorded them jumping half a dozen times, I started to wonder, *When am I going to watch that video?* When I'm in my sixties and the kids are in their forties, are we really going to pull up the file and watch them jump off a Kirkland park bench in slow motion?

Why does that deserve slow motion, anyway? I'm a child of the '80s, and I remember when slow motion was reserved for replays of Michael Jordan on game day. Now my pre-teens are jumping one foot straight down—also known as *falling*—and I'm cheering them on and recording the moment for posterity. And it's in slow motion, in case they want to analyze their form later.

I really don't take too many slow-motion videos, because they are just . . . too slow. I have a short attention span. And I don't do time lapse, because I always get it wrong. I don't time things properly, and I end up with jerky videos with no one in them.

Without a doubt, my favorite option is panorama. Taking panoramic pictures is a game to me. Why? Because when you select *pano* on an iPhone, a straight line and an arrow appear on the screen, and you have to pan the phone while keeping the arrow on the line. I'm totally down for anything that involves competition, even if it's seeing how fast and level I can move my phone. I love it.

Besides the game factor, I love panoramic because you get an awesome perspective. Sure, the end result looks a little warped, and anyone who moves during the picture gets morphed into an alien blob. But a panorama is still amazing because it captures the entire scene and experience in one shot. You see more in the picture than you do in real life.

How great would it be to have a panoramic option when it comes to our lives? It's far too easy to get fixated on our present circumstances and lose sight of the bigger picture. We get stressed out and terrified because what we are facing seems overwhelming. Needless to say, that is not a healthy place for our souls to stay for long. What if we could somehow go up to the 30,000-foot level and see the beginning, middle, and end of any given situation?

There are certainly times in life when, with a bit of effort and self-control, we gain a better perspective. I highly recommend that, of course. The bigger our perspective, the better equipped we will be to face the ups and downs of life. There are other times, however, when no matter how hard we try, we can't see a way out of our problems. What then? How do our souls gain perspective in the middle of impossible circumstances?

That is where God comes in. God never gets overwhelmed, because unlike you and me, he can see the entire panorama of our lives all at once. He doesn't just see what we are currently facing—he sees how we are going to get through it and how we will be better people because of it. That's perspective.

One of my favorite moments in the life of Jesus was when he and his disciples were crossing the Sea of Galilee and a huge storm came out of nowhere. The disciples were panicking and rowing, rowing and panicking. Meanwhile, Jesus was asleep on a pillow in the back of the boat. Mark records that the disciples woke him up, shouting, "Teacher, don't you care that we're going to drown?" (Mark 4:38 NLT).

Jesus addressed the wind and waves, "Silence! Be still!" (verse 39 NLT). The wind ceased; the sea became calm. At this point the disciples were even more freaked out than before. "Who is this man?" They stared at each other in shock. "Even the wind and waves obey him!" (verse 41 NLT).

The disciples could only see the storm, so they panicked. Jesus could see beyond the storm, so he was able to sleep through it. The difference was perspective.

Jesus' attitude of peace and quiet confidence in the middle of the storm was a message to the disciples. He was preaching to them from his pillow. Rather than depending on their limited viewpoint, they should have trusted in his perspective.

Here's what I've found. I don't have to know the way out of my storm. I don't have to know the future. I just have to know the one who anchors and sustains my soul: Jesus. No matter what storm I might be going through, Jesus is with me. He isn't overwhelmed or afraid. He has his eye on my future, and as long as my eyes are on him, my soul can be at peace.

- What storms or difficult situations are you currently experiencing?

- Why is it often hard to have a complete perspective or see the whole picture when you are in the middle of a storm?

- How does knowing that Jesus sees the entire panorama help your soul find rest and peace?

EXPANDING GOD

In my experience, there are essentially two types of communicators: expanders and condensers. You can't be both. Either you tend to expand and expound on every detail, or you reduce everything to its shortest possible explanation.

I am an expander, in case you were wondering. Actually,

you could call me an extreme expander. I have no problem with that—I love being an expander. I think expanders have way more fun.

All condensers care about are facts. Expanders, however, care about feelings. Condensers want to make a point. Expanders want to make friends. Condensers start talking only when absolutely necessary. Expanders *stop* talking only when absolutely necessary.

You know you are an expander when you start talking before you even know what you are going to say, because it's not really about the topic—it's about talking. An expander's idea of listening is waiting for his or her turn to talk.

There is nothing like two expanders going to coffee together. It's a party. There are multiple conversations happening at once. There is no such thing as "awkward" silence when two expanders get together, because there is no silence at all. But have you ever seen two condensers go out for coffee?

"How was your week?"

"Good. Yours?"

"Same."

"Plans this weekend?"

"Golf."

"Nice."

"Yep."

"Great talk. Bye."

How boring is that?

I am especially grateful to be an expander in my role as husband. It serves me well. If you are a husband and a condenser, God be with you, because at some point your wife will ask one of those lose-lose questions, such as, "Does this look good on me?" And as a condenser, you will give her a straight answer: "No, not at all."

I guarantee you, that will not end well.

As an expander, though, I would reply, "Does it look good on you? Babe, honestly, I love yellow. One of my favorite colors. I've never seen you in yellow, but yellow is like sunshine, which we don't get a lot of in Seattle, so that's awesome. I think you look great in a lot of colors. I obviously think blue is your best color, but yellow is cool. Does it look good on you? I don't know, but I think *you* are amazing. I love you. I think you are awesome. . . . Oh, you want to change and wear a different dress? Great! You absolutely should."

I'm winning, right?

If you are a condenser, don't feel bad—the Bible tends to condense things, too. In this case, though, it's not because of a lack of things to say. The opposite is true. The truths the Bible reveals about God are so profound and their implications are so far-reaching that it's impossible to fully explain them on the written page.

That's why Jesus came to Earth. He didn't come to tell us about God, because words would not be enough. Jesus is God is human form, and he came to show us in tangible, visible ways who God is. He came to expand our concept of God. Jesus exemplified in day-to-day, real-life scenarios what God's love and forgiveness and grace look like. Paul wrote this about Jesus:

> *Christ is the visible image of the invisible God.*
> *He existed before anything was created and is supreme*

> *over all creation. . . .*
> *For God in all his fullness*
> *was pleased to live in Christ,*
> *and through him God reconciled*
> *everything to himself.*
> *He made peace with everything in heaven and on earth*
> *by means of Christ's blood on the cross.*
> (Colossians 1:15, 19–20 NLT)

In other words, Jesus was God living among humanity. Not only that, but Jesus was also God's plan to restore humanity to himself. Jesus came to show us God and to bring us back to God.

What does all this have to do with our souls? Just this: our souls need to anchor themselves to someone bigger than us. When we find ourselves adrift and alone, we realize our need for a savior. For a rescuer. For someone or something big enough and strong enough to bring us stability.

If our view of God is that he is disinterested, or vengeful, or fickle, or impossible to please, we will have a tough time trusting him. Rather than turning to God as the anchor for our souls, we will look for things we think are less likely to turn against us. After all, how can we trust in a God who is against us or doesn't care about us?

Enter Jesus.

For three and a half years, Jesus roamed the ancient land of Israel in a robe and sandals, just doing life with a group of ordinary—maybe even below ordinary—guys. Along the way, he showed us how much God loves people living with hurt. He

showed us God's power to change even the most impossible circumstances. He showed us how quick God is to forgive sinners.

Jesus came to expand our view and experience of God. I find
that incredibly encouraging. God isn't out to impress us with his
mysteriousness. He doesn't want us to live in fear or confusion,
always wondering if we are good enough to be accepted. He isn't
aloof and alone, far removed from our needs and weaknesses.

God is right in the middle of our mess. He cares enough and
is strong enough to aid us. Jesus proved this when he lived, died,
and rose again in full view of people just like you and me.

If you need help unpacking what the Bible says about God,
just read what it says about Jesus, and let your soul find hope.

- Do you ever wonder what God thinks about you? Do you
  tend to think he is happy or angry with you? That he is
  pleased or disappointed?

- How does the life of Jesus help you visualize and
  understand God's attitude toward you?

- What do you think Jesus would tell you if you could talk to him in person? How would he react to your needs, your mistakes, and your dreams?

THE ILLUSION OF CONTROL

I fly a lot. Because our church has campuses in Seattle, Los Angeles, and Guadalajara, Mexico, I find myself navigating the unique domain of airlines far more often than I'd like.

I've made my peace with that reality, so I do much of my sermon prep in the air. Alaska Airlines is my mobile office. Usually, I'll wear a hoodie so no one recognizes me, throw on some headphones, and focus on my notes the whole flight. It's nothing personal—I'm just not great at making small talk with complete strangers who are sharing my arm space and breathing out particles that I have to breathe in.

Recently, I had an experience during a flight that left a deep impact on me. I mentioned it in the video teaching for this week's session. I was on a plane from Seattle to LA, and the guy next to me was clearly a high-powered executive. He had the suit, the laptop, and the attitude. Before we had even taken off, he was already typing furiously.

I caught his eye as I sat down, and I could see him take in my hoodie and ripped jeans. I didn't look professional or successful or probably even employed. His face and body language couldn't have been clearer: I didn't measure up. He scooted over slightly and started typing more furiously.

I didn't really mind. I pulled my hood up, got out my notebook, and jumped back into studying for a message I was preaching that night. My notes are like my brain: random, colorful, and full of cartoon illustrations. I caught Mr. Laptop looking at my notebook scribbles. He didn't seem to approve of those, either. His aloofness was palpable.

Then out of nowhere, a few minutes before we landed in LA, we hit the worst turbulence I've ever experienced. I am not exaggerating. It was terrifying. I've been on some crazy flights and survived a few genuinely dangerous landings, but this turbulence was next level. The plane dropped probably a hundred feet instantly, and then started bouncing all over the place. Drinks were spilling, people were screaming, and even the flight attendants were panicking. That's a really bad sign, by the way. Usually when you hit bumpy weather and you look over at them, they are calmly solving Sudoku puzzles, and you feel dumb for even thinking the plane was in trouble. Not this time.

In a matter of seconds, that executive went from being in control and aloof to whimpering like a frightened poodle. I could see his knuckles turning white around his armrests. His cries got louder and louder with each jolt and drop.

I can't criticize him: I was scared too, as was everyone else on that flight. But someone told me once that no plane has ever gone down due to turbulence, and I guess I believed him. Plus, I was really getting a lot out of my study session. I was having a genuine moment with God. So for maybe the only time in my life, I was the emotionally stable person in the situation. It felt *amazing*. And if we're being honest here, I might have experienced a bit of sadistic pleasure watching the executive's aloofness evaporate.

We landed safely, and the passengers gave the pilot an ovation. It would have been a standing ovation, but the seat belt light was still on.

For some reason, that experience really affected me. I thought about it for days. There is nothing like absolute helplessness to make you evaluate what your soul holds on to or where you get your sense of security.

The logical way to find security is to be more in control. It's to plan for every contingency and provide for every possibility. It's to work hard now so the future is guaranteed, to cross our *I*s, dot our *T*s, and make sure our retirement is fully funded. But that logic leads us astray. Not that hard work or retirement plans are bad, but all it takes is an unexpected bout of turbulence to show us how illusory self-based security is.

My businessman seat partner was a great illustration of that. Again, I don't judge him. His reaction was understandable. I've been there many times. But my soul felt strangely at peace on that flight. Even though my emotions—and my stomach—were all over the place, my soul was not. It was stable and secure.

Why? I asked myself that question over the next few days. What helped my soul trust and relax even when the circumstances around me were genuinely terrifying? The answer I came to was simply this: I know that God is in control of my soul. I know my life is in his hands. My soul can hold fast to him no matter what external turbulence or craziness I might be facing.

In the ancient writings of Isaiah, God told Israel: "Only in returning to me and resting in me will you be saved. In quietness and confidence is your strength" (Isaiah 30:15 NLT).

Our souls find help not in control, but in returning to God; not in outward guarantees, but in inward trust. Our hope is in God. We access true rest, salvation, and strength by allowing our souls to hold on to him.

That doesn't mean our thoughts and emotions won't fluctuate. They will. I can guarantee it. I may never again be the emotionally stable person in a situation. But despite outward turbulence, our souls can be secure. Our souls find help and strength in God.

- How do you feel when you are out of control in an area of your life? How do you tend to react in those moments?

- How easy is it for you to trust God? Are there some areas that are harder than others?

- Why does trusting that God is in control ultimately bring more peace to your soul than trying to be in control yourself?

HOW IS MY SOUL HELPED?

WELCOME

Welcome to the fifth session of *How's Your Soul?* Last week, we discussed how Jesus is our anchor no matter what storm we might face. He gives our souls the stability and safety they need.

This week, we want to answer the question, "How is my soul helped?" We will look at two primary sources of help: staying surrendered and staying surrounded. Both are simple yet essential sources of assistance.

We can't predict or control what life might bring our way, but we can ensure that our souls stay in a surrendered, surrounded environment. Let's look at these two terms in more detail through this week's video teaching.

VIDEO TEACHING

The following are a few key thoughts to note as you watch session five of the video. Use the space provided to jot down personal observations or applications.

The apostle Paul experienced more than his share of struggles and pain. Yet his writings portray a man whose soul was buoyant and alive. He lived a flourishing and effective life.

In 1 Corinthians 16, we see two sources of help illustrated in the life of Paul that can allow our souls to thrive.

The first source of help can be seen in the number of times that Paul says things like "perhaps" and "if the Lord wills." Paul reveals here that his schedule, his agenda, and his priorities are subject to God. In other words, a healthy soul is a *surrendered* soul.

The only alternative to a surrendered life is carrying all the weight and pressure ourselves. That is not a healthy place for our souls to be. But when we yield control to God, we are able to cast our cares on him and depend on him.

The second source of help for our souls can be seen in the number of individuals who Paul mentions by name in 1 Corinthians 16. This illustrates the importance of staying *surrounded*.

It's easy to allow life to isolate us, but that is dangerous for our souls. Our souls were designed to flourish in conjunction and cooperation with other people.

When we intentionally live surrendered and surrounded lives, we find the help our souls need. It's not always easy to live this way, but it is worth it.

GROUP DISCUSSION

Take a few minutes to discuss the following questions with your group.

1. What are some areas in your life that are hard for you to surrender to God? Why are they more difficult than other areas?

2. The apostle Peter wrote, "Give all your worries and cares to God, for he cares about you" (1 Peter 5:7 NLT). How does the knowledge that God cares help you surrender your worries to him?

3. How does surrender help your soul stay healthy, sane, and stable?

4. Is it easy or hard for you to make friends? Do only certain personality types need friends, or do all of us need them? Explain.

5. How does staying surrounded help your soul stay grounded and healthy?

6. What are some practical ways to ensure you live a surrounded life?

CLOSING PRAYER

Close your time together in prayer. Here are a few ideas of what you could pray about based on the topic of this session:

- Pray that God would help you surrender your life and trust him completely, especially in areas that are more difficult for you to yield control.
- Pray for healthy friendships and for relationships that restore and protect your soul.
- Pray that even when relationships are difficult or you find yourself hurt, you would not isolate yourself.
- Pray that you would also help others by being the friend their souls need.

WEEKLY CHALLENGE

Take time this week to honestly evaluate how surrendered and surrounded you are, keeping in mind that these two areas will help your soul flourish and thrive.

Surrendered: Spend a few minutes in prayer once or twice over the next few days and ask the Holy Spirit to show you if there are any areas of your life where you have not yielded control. Remember, the more you are able to surrender, the more your soul will be able to rest and grow.

Surrounded: What personal struggles or dreams have you kept hidden inside? Decide on one area that you want to share with a trusted friend, and find time this week to be authentic and transparent with that person.

RECOMMENDED READING

Review chapters 5 and 7 in the book *How's Your Soul?* Use the space provided to write any key points or questions you want to bring to the next group meeting.

Personal Study

Session 5

GREATER THAN MY HEART

Can you remember your least favorite job? I actually haven't had that many jobs, so this is not a hard question for me. My first job was a part-time employee at a golf course. I got free golf out of the deal, so that was definitely not my least favorite. Currently—and probably until I retire—I am a pastor, which I also love.

But sandwiched between golfing and pastoring, I was employed as a church custodian. It was the church my parents started and pastored at the time, the City Church, which I now pastor. Being a church custodian was, without a doubt, my least favorite job.

Specifically, I had a tough time with the Sunday night shift. Our building measures 133,000 square feet. It has three wings consisting of a main auditorium, a couple of smaller auditoriums, countless classrooms and offices, and more bathrooms and toilets than a stadium. At the time, we had a couple thousand people attending every Sunday, spread out over services that took place throughout the day.

There were usually three of us assigned to the Sunday night shift. Once all the services were over and quiet had descended on the campus, we would survey the damage. I remember standing in the lobby, vacuum cleaners strapped to our backs like a trio of Ghostbusters, stunned by the carnage we were responsible to clean up.

While we cleaned, we'd listen to music and sermons. We'd have rap battles. We'd flip coins to see who had to clean the women's restrooms. And sometime in the wee hours of the morning, we would finally finish.

Then one week later, the place would be trashed again. After the cars drove off, we'd strap on our vacuum cleaners and start over. This happened week after week after painful week. That cycle only had to repeat itself a few times before I found something strange happening to me. I started to resent having so many people in "my" building. I'd watch someone toss a paper cup at a garbage can, miss, and then walk off. And inside I'd think, *Seriously? Why don't you clean up after yourself there, slugger?*

I would see a line outside the women's restroom and be like, *There's a line? This is getting out of control. This is insane. Dear God, Lord, take me now. Where are Cinderella's mice? Can they help?*

It started to feel overwhelming. *Again? I can't do this all over. It's too much. And it will just get messy again.*

Maybe you've felt that feeling of frustration and hopelessness when surveying your own soul. I know I have. It's human nature. In our spiritual journey, we work hard to fix ourselves, to clean ourselves up, to improve and advance.

"I'm really going to follow Jesus," we say. "I'm finally going to be the spiritual person I want to be. I'll be disciplined and focused and moral and pure. I'm going to start attending church. I'm going to underline verses in my Bible. I'm going to clean up my life."

And then, in one night, all our progress is undone. With one bad decision, we are back where we started. We cleaned 133,000 square feet of heart and soul, and now it's a mess again. In those moments, we sometimes find ourselves thinking, *This is too much. I can't do this again. It's two steps forward and two—or three—steps back. I'm just not cut out for this.*

The apostle John, one of Jesus' disciples and closest friends, seems to have understood that feeling of frustration very well. He wrote this: "By this we shall know that we are of the truth and reassure our heart before him; for whenever our heart condemns us, God is greater than our heart, and he knows everything" (1 John 3:19–20).

I can't tell you how encouraging the little phrase "God is greater than our heart" is to me. John is saying that even when our souls are condemned, frustrated, and overwhelmed, God is greater. His love is greater, his grace is greater, and his power is greater. He is not overwhelmed by our messes, nor does he give up on us just because we don't seem to be making any progress.

As humans we tend to judge our success (and therefore our value) based on our progress. We measure that progress using self-defined criteria. So if we haven't kicked the dog or yelled at the kids today, we are doing well. If we haven't looked at online pornography late at night, we are making progress.

The problem is, those criteria are relative and subjective. They are based on comparing ourselves to who we used to be, or who we want to be, or who someone else thinks we should be. They evaluate external actions, not internal attitudes.

Besides that, we are assuming that what God really values is improvement. We think that God is about behavior modification, that he will be happier with us or love us more if we clean up a few more of our messes.

That approach to God is even more demotivating than cleaning up after two thousand church attenders. It's no wonder our souls feel overwhelmed at times. We think following God is about staying perfectly clean or about never failing. Let's be honest, though. Our souls and hearts don't exist behind museum glass. We don't live in a sanitized, sterilized, mess-free world. We are going to fail from time to time.

And God is okay with that. He already provided the means for forgiveness: Jesus. And he gives us grace to face each day anew: again, through Jesus. Our stance before God is secure, because even if our souls condemn us, God is greater. One bad decision or weak moment can't change our relationship with God. Our addictions don't shake heaven. Our marriage troubles or financial missteps or anger management issues don't change God's theology. Nothing is greater than God. Therefore, nothing can take us from his arms.

What helps your heart be strong? Who helps your soul be confident? Not good works or self-righteousness or emotions. You can't talk yourself or work yourself into a state of confidence.

Your soul finds stability in Jesus' finished work. If you believe in Jesus, then you are righteous. You are accepted, forgiven, and loved. His hand is on your life, and he won't let go. God gives you permission to get back up, no matter how many times you've fallen. God is greater than your soul, so your soul can find its confidence and help in him.

- Do you tend to deal with feelings of guilt or doubt? What circumstances or situations trigger those feelings?

- How do you usually handle failure?

- How can knowing that God is greater than your emotions, fears, and messes help you deal with the ups and downs of life?

ALL TERRAIN FAITH

A while back, in a moment of misguided manhood, I decided to buy an ATV. To be honest, I didn't know or care what "ATV" stood for. All I wanted was a souped-up golf cart I could look cool in as I drove around our neighborhood.

My first mistake was not looking up the meaning of ATV. My second was not telling Chelsea that I was going to buy it. But that's another story. Anyway, I found an ATV website, and after a bit of looking, I found the deal of a lifetime. I saved thousands of dollars—or at least that's what they told me.

A few days later, the ATV showed up. Naturally, I had included a license plate for it: BLEZZED. I was pumped. I couldn't wait. Chelsea said, "It's ugly. I hate it. I hate it like you hate cats."

I was like, "There's no way you hate it that much."

Once I figured out how to put gas in it, which only took me three hours, I set out on my maiden voyage. I drove up and down the streets around our house, trying to get a feel for this machine.

Something seemed wrong, though. The engine ran too loud and rough. The gears felt jerky. I even thought maybe the e-brake was on, but it wasn't. I started to wonder if I'd saved thousands of dollars on a lemon. Several days later, some friends came over. I asked a couple of the guys if they'd take a look at my ATV. So we went out on the road. After driving it for a few minutes, one of them said, "Judah, it's fine. This is how it's supposed to run."

"But it's rough and jerky."

"What are you talking about? It's perfect."

"Then why is it so bumpy when I drive down the street? Why is it so loud?"

My friends looked at me funny. "Judah, do you know what this is? Do you know what an ATV is for?"

I said, "It's like a golf cart, right? Except cool?"

They said, "ATV stands for *All Terrain Vehicle*. This was made for off-road use, not for streets. Look, it has roll bars. It has straps. It has seatbelts. This thing is a beast."

I said, "Off-road use? I'm not going to do that. Ever."

My friends ignored me. They found a dirt road, and we hit the trails. We "rallied," to use the lingo. And sure enough, that ATV was in its element. Dirt was flying, grasshoppers were scattering, and my friends were yelling.

I hated every second of it. "I feel dusty," I told them. So now, the ATV mostly sits in my driveway, except for when I putter around the paved, lighted, pothole-free streets near my house.

Sometimes I think we want the same thing from our faith and our relationship with Jesus that I wanted from my vehicle. We want safe, quiet, and controlled lives. We want to stay on the road. Risk? Forget it. Adventure? Thank you, but no. Unpredictability? Too scary.

And yet our faith is made for off-road use, and our souls are designed to yield to God's control. Only in surrender will we truly find security and health for our souls.

We were created to follow Jesus around hairpin turns and along breathtaking cliffs. Life with Jesus is an adventure, and we'll be frustrated if we think he'll always keep us on the road. Rather than fighting what we were made for, we need to embrace it. We need to surrender to God's control and God's design for our lives.

God is completely trustworthy, and that is why we can follow his lead with full confidence. I love how Proverbs 3:5–6 puts it:

> *Trust God from the bottom of your heart;*
> *don't try to figure out everything on your own.*
> *Listen for God's voice in everything you do, everywhere you go;*
> *he's the one who will keep you on track.* (MSG)

Our tendency to hope for a safe, secure life is usually rooted in fear. We want to control our environment because, we think, that's the only way to guarantee nothing bad will happen. Yet control is an illusion, as anyone who has lived on this planet for a few decades has probably figured out. Things like money, intelligence, education, and connections are a great advantage, and they can give us the feeling we have life figured out. But all it takes is an economic downturn, political upheaval, or personal tragedy to make us realize our lives are far more fragile than we'd like to think.

The safest life is not hunkering down and holding on to what's ours. It's not trying to plan every moment or foresee every detail of the future. On an emotional level that might sound great, but our souls need more than superficial safety. They need the security and peace that come from Jesus. The safest life, therefore, is one that surrenders to and embraces the spontaneous, unpredictable adventure inherent in following Jesus.

Do you feel that following God has put you in a difficult place?

Do you feel frustrated or confused because your faith doesn't seem to be working right? Did you expect this lifestyle of following Jesus to be a bit easier or smoother?

I don't think the problem is that your faith isn't working—I think it's working just the way it was created to. True faith will lead you into decisions, lifestyles, and relationships that don't always feel safe. That's okay. Faith isn't about avoiding danger or playing it safe. It isn't about staying comfortable. Faith is about *Jesus*. Your soul is built for adventure, for following Jesus no matter what, for living a life of great risk and great rewards.

Your faith was made for this. And when you follow Jesus, you will find both true adventure and ultimate security.

- Do you ever find yourself wishing life were easier or safer? What do you think is at the root of that desire?

- Is it hard for you to surrender your life to God? Why or why not? How does surrender actually help your soul be more secure?

- What does it mean to you that your faith is meant to go "off-road"?

FIRST FIGHT

I still remember the first fight Chelsea and I had as a married couple. We had only fought once before, when we were dating, and that was over a Bible verse (of all things).

This was our first real fight, though. It happened about a week after our honeymoon. In retrospect that's not a great start, but we've been married seventeen years and counting, so obviously things worked out.

I should mention that I lived with my parents right up until my wedding day. I was twenty-one when I got married, and I had never lived on my own. There was no process of separation, no exploration of independence. I literally moved out of my house and moved in with Chelsea. My parents helped us purchase a duplex that happened to be 0.8 miles from their house.

I love my parents. That's good, right? So even after the wedding and honeymoon, we saw a lot of each other. They came over every day, in fact. Unannounced. Usually bearing gifts, or opinions, or both.

One day, my bride said we needed to talk. I was naive. I had no idea that was code for, "You are doing something stupid that needs to change."

What she said was, "Are your parents going to come over every day?"

It was a loaded question. It was a rhetorical question. Unfortunately, I tried to answer it at face value. "Well, yes? Or, no? I mean, not *every* day. Unless they want to. Is that a problem? They are just trying to help. I owe them a lot, you know."

That didn't go over well. She explained what she meant: she loved my family, but she married me, not them. I was married to her now, and she needed her space and her husband.

But I took it personally. I found myself getting emotional—no surprise there. I started making and defending points I didn't even believe. In retrospect it was silly, like most fights are. But in the moment, the emotional struggle was deep, and it was real.

After the argument was over and we reached some sort of ceasefire, I remember going into another room and thinking, *I don't know if this is going to work for me. I thought marriage would be love and happy feelings and frequent lovemaking. But this? I didn't sign up for this. This is hard!*

We laugh about it now, but both of us—maybe mostly me—approached the marriage relationship thinking it would be fairly easy. That being in love was enough. That butterflies and hormones would carry us through. Then we discovered the other spouse had opinions that didn't always agree with ours. We found out that miscommunication and hurt feelings and selfish motives are part of any relationship—even sincere, godly, committed ones.

I'd love to say that after a certain number of years, relational conflict is no longer an issue. But even though we love each other more than ever, and even though we understand and value one another like never before, we still have to work at this thing called *relationship*.

Recently, someone sent me an article about an interview Chelsea had done. The interviewer had asked some questions about our marriage. Chelsea answered candidly, because she is Chelsea and that's how she answers. The headline read: "Pastor Judah Smith's Wife Chelsea Says 'Marriage Is Hard.'"

I was like, "Really, Chels? That's how you bottom-lined it? When did you even do that interview? Were you like up late at night after I fell asleep, whispering desperately into the phone, 'It's so hard being married to Judah. Really—you have no idea what I go through.'"

She just laughed. But she didn't tell me otherwise.

Despite the difficult moments, despite the mistakes and misunderstandings, my marriage is the most fulfilling, enjoyable, stabilizing element of my life outside of my walk with Jesus. And I'm pretty sure the same is true for Chelsea—regardless of that headline. We were made for each other. We are better together. Our souls find help and strength in one another.

The same holds true for relationships in general. *Our souls need to be surrounded by other people.* None of us was created to be alone or to face life alone. We need companionship, relationship, and encouragement. We are better together, because our souls find help when they need it the most.

Yes, relationships can be tricky. They can be messy and

painful. They can blow up in our faces, leaving us hurt and lonely. But that doesn't mean we should give up, build tree forts in Montana, and live alone the rest of our lives. It doesn't mean we should isolate ourselves emotionally from other people as protection against further hurt. The apostle Paul wrote:

Since God chose you to be the holy people he loves, you must clothe yourselves with tenderhearted mercy, kindness, humility, gentleness, and patience. Make allowance for each other's faults, and forgive anyone who offends you. Remember, the Lord forgave you, so you must forgive others. Above all, clothe yourselves with love, which binds us all together in perfect harmony.

(Colossians 3:12–14 NLT)

The point is clear: relationships take work. They require patience, forgiveness, and humility. *But they are worth it.* Imagine a community where this kind of love-based, grace-filled relationship is the norm. Who wouldn't thrive there?

Paul goes on to detail the nuances of several interpersonal relationships, including marriage, children and parents, and employees and bosses. He doesn't hide from the reality of interpersonal conflict. Instead, he shows how following Jesus will naturally produce healthy relationships.

God wants to surround your soul with healthy, life-giving relationships. He wants to be at the center of your marriage, your parenting, and your friendships. He designed your soul to function best when it is encircled by a community of people who are committed to your well-being and with whom you can share your life. There may be rocky moments along the way, but it is worth it in the long run.

- Who are some of your closest friends? How do they contribute to your life?

- Have you ever experienced deep loneliness? How does that affect your soul over time?

- Who are some people in your world who you could improve your relationship with? What would be a practical first step?

WHERE IS MY SOUL HEADED?

WELCOME

Welcome to the final session of *How's Your Soul?* It's been a revealing—and hopefully healing—journey of discovery, and it's only the beginning. God wants to lead, shape, and protect your soul for the rest of your life.

This week, we will answer the question, "Where is my soul headed?" We'll talk about what we want our lives to look like years down the road, and how that picture should influence how we live today.

Ultimately, of course, our souls' destination is heaven. This life is not just about this life—it's about Jesus, and it's about eternity with God.

Our dreams for this life and the reality of heaven in the next life both play a significant role in our lives today. As we watch this week's video teaching, let's focus on how we can shape our present in light of what is ahead.

VIDEO TEACHING

The following are a few key thoughts to note as you watch session six of the video. Use the space provided to jot down personal observations or applications.

If we allow hurts and disappoints to affect our souls, we can find ourselves at the end of our lives alone and closed off. It's a natural desire for self-preservation, but in the long run, it is not where we want to end up.

We need to ask ourselves how we want our lives to end up and where we are headed.

How we want to be at the end of our lives should shape how we live in the present.

Our soul is like a circle. We can either make that circle smaller or larger over the course of our lives.

Rather than closing in a little bit more each time we are hurt, we need to continually forgive people. God designed us to be big people; he created us to be proponents of forgiveness, mercy, and grace.

Jesus is the best big circle drawer in history. He invites anyone and everyone to come to him and receive from him.

We need to adopt the same attitude as Jesus. We want to live, look, and love like Jesus.

GROUP DISCUSSION

Take a few minutes to discuss the following questions with your group.

1. Have you ever been deeply hurt in a relationship? How did that affect you?

2. What is the end result of a life that constantly gets smaller with each hurt, disappointment, or tragedy?

3. How can you keep your soul from getting smaller and smaller?

4. Why is forgiveness necessary for your soul?

5. How did Jesus model a big, generous, accepting soul?

6. What do you want your life to look like at the end? How does that picture affect how you live now?

CLOSING PRAYER

Close your time together in prayer. Here are a few ideas of what you could pray about based on the topic of this session:

- Pray that God would help you forgive people who have hurt you.
- Pray that your soul would get bigger and bigger, and that you would be the generous, loving person God created you to be.
- Pray that you would find the rest and acceptance Jesus offers, and that you would be able to adopt the same attitude he has in your relationships with others.
- Pray that at the end of your life, you will live, love, and look like Jesus.

WEEKLY CHALLENGE

Find some time this week for a bit of deep soul-searching. Look back over your life, starting with your childhood all the way up to the present. Make a note (in your head or on paper, whatever you prefer) of times your soul was deeply hurt. The goal here is not to relive the experiences or feel hurt all over again, but simply to recognize the reality of the pain.

Then take your list and give it to God. Spend a few moments in prayer asking God to take control of the emotions, the memories, and the consequences of those experiences. Allow him to heal your soul and lead you to a place where you can truly forgive.

On another day, take a few moments to write down what you want your loved ones to say about you at the end of your life. What kind of person do you want to be? What do you want your values to be?

In light of your goal, what changes can you make right now? Is the way you are using your time, energy, and resources going to take you where you want to go?

RECOMMENDED READING

Review chapters 8 through 10 in *How's Your Soul?* Use the space provided to write any key points or questions you want to discuss with either someone from your group or a family member or friend in the days ahead.

Final Personal Study

RHYTHMS AND PROGRESS

As a family, we are officially out of diaper season. That's a big deal, as you know if you have small children. I hated the diaper season. Am I allowed to admit that? I hated it wholeheartedly. Just because I'm a parent, do I have to enjoy every part of parenting? Honestly, I never want to get comfortable with human waste, and I think that's okay.

The whole process is just bizarre. For example, have you ever used the smell method to see if a diaper needed changing? When you are in the diaper season, you don't think about how gross that is. You might be at a mall, and everyone is watching as you pick up your two-year-old, put your nose in the vicinity of his backside, and inhale. "He's good! Carry on!" Really? How is the poor kid supposed to be human again?

Or you pull back the waistband and check visually. "No, must have just been gas," you announce loudly. And everyone cheers, and you push off toward another store. Did you ever consider how the kid must feel? *What am I, Dad, just a waste factory? I have feelings too.*

As a married couple, you develop strategies to get your spouse to change the diaper. The classic one is just ignoring it, because whoever smells it first is contractually obligated to take care of it. So Chelsea would ask me, "Judah, do you smell something?"

Of course I did. All of Nordstrom's could smell it. "No, not at all. Why, do you? Maybe you should check the baby."

Was I pretending? Yes. Is pretending a form of lying? Um, you can just shut up now.

It's the same kind of lying you do when the kids wake up in the middle of the night and you pretend you are fast asleep. Chelsea says, "Judah. Judah? Judah!" She tries all forms of punctuation, but I just lie there like I'm totally out.

The next morning, she says, "I was up for forty-five minutes with the kids."

I'm like, "Oh my gosh, I am so sorry! I was so out of it. You should have woken me up. Wish I could have been there for you."

"Judah, that's lying." Yeah, but God forgives me, so don't judge me.

There is one aspect of diaper season I loved, though. It was when they were just beginning to hold themselves up against a couch or coffee table. If you've had kids, you know what I'm talking about. They can't walk, they can't talk, but they stand there in nothing but their little Huggies, and their skin is so soft and pinchable. I know it's weird, but you just wish you could eat them.

Then—and this happened with all three of my kids—you put on music. And they stand with their shaky legs and giant diaper caboose, and they begin moving to the music. Their little buns start bumping to the beat. Tell me that's not one of the cutest things you have ever seen.

You get out your camera, because obviously this kid is a prodigy. He's got music in him. He's the next Beethoven. "Chelsea, come look! It's amazing!"

Of course, every human has done this, but you just think your child is special. There is nothing cuter than that little one swaying and moving and dancing. It's adorable, and it's proof that rhythm is within us.

We were designed with rhythm, and we were designed to live in an environment of rhythm and routine and pace. God, the rhythm maker, made our hearts to beat regularly. He designed night and day. He designed minutes and moments, hours and days, weeks and months and years. There is a beginning to things and there is an end to things.

God could have created us without the element of time. Have you ever thought about that? He could have created a universe with no rhythm, no resolve, no movement. We could have existed in some ethereal, eternal state where nothing changes or grows, where nothing is born and nothing dies.

God didn't do that, though. We have new days, new dawns, and new seasons. Kids start out as babies, progress through diaper season, survive junior high, learn to drive, and eventually become adults. This is all designed by God, and it tells us that rhythm, pace, and progress are essential to a healthy soul.

On a soul level, we were not created to just exist. We are not sucking oxygen on this planet to merely survive. Our souls are headed somewhere, both in this life and in the life to come. God has a plan and a future for us, and our souls will be healthiest when we allow God to lead us into the future he has planned.

Philippians 1:6 is one of the most encouraging verses in the Bible on this topic. Paul wrote to the church in the ancient city of Philippi, "I am certain that God, who began the good work within you, will continue his work until it is finally finished on the day when Christ Jesus returns" (NLT).

The first thing to note about this verse is that it is *God* who began the work. That internal, innate drive to accomplish specific things in life comes from God. He wants you to find fulfillment and achieve success even more than you do. You and I are free to pursue *his* plans *his* way, because ultimately he is the one who started the work to begin with.

Then Paul says the good work began "within you." In other words, God's plan for your life is first and foremost an *inside job*. He wants to transform your soul. He wants to heal your soul. He wants to free your soul. A healthy inside will naturally produce a healthy outside, so God begins his work in your mind, will, heart, and emotions.

The final thing to note is that the same God who *began* the work will both *continue* and *finish* it. That's easy to believe when your progress is evident, but it's a lot harder when you seem to be sliding backward faster than you are moving forward. If God began the work, you can be confident he will finish it. You don't have to architect your destiny. You don't have to guarantee your success. You just have to align yourself with the work God is already doing within you, and he will be faithful to finish it.

Your soul is headed for health and success in Jesus, and he is with you every season and stage of the journey.

- In what areas of your life have you seen significant progress? How have you been aware of God helping you in those areas?

- Are there things in your life that don't seem to change? How does that make you feel?

- How does knowing that God is in charge of the rhythms, pace, and progress of your soul help you deal with potentially frustrating areas of personal growth?

END IN MIND

My dad had a set of stock phrases that seem to have stuck with me, because I find myself saying them to my kids. For example, I heard this growing up: "What goes up must come down." Really? Who came up with that one? That's called *gravity*. But somehow it is ingrained in our collective cultural conscience, and we repeat it solemnly, as if it explains one of life's greatest mysteries.

Or how about this one: "No pain, no gain." My dad had his own version: "No pain, no pain." I couldn't agree with my dad more, actually. In general, I am against pain. Gain is overrated if it hurts that much. Someone asked me once if I do cross fit. I said, "No, because I don't want to hurt."

Here's another cliché my dad liked: "It's not how you start—it's how you finish." One of the first times I remember hearing that sentiment was in third grade. I went to a small Christian school, and it had an annual fundraiser that pretty much revolved around children being forced to run around a track for money. Yes, it was as bad as it sounds. The idea was to solicit donations from friends, family, and neighbors based on how many times we ran around the school track. I guess the idea was that people would feel so sorry for us they'd pay money to ease their conscience.

I recall lining up with the other kids for a race. I was by no means a track star, and when you are eight or nine years old, that track looks enormous. But one thing I always had going for me was a high level of self-confidence, and I had no doubt that I would defeat the entire field of competitors.

The starting gun fired, and I immediately shot into the lead. I remember looking back at the pack of third graders lagging behind and thinking I might actually be the fastest human in history.

Then about halfway around the first lap, something bizarre happened. They all passed me. I couldn't understand why suddenly I was so slow. When the race was over, I had finished dead last. I wept bitterly, because I was emotionally unstable as a child. Not much has changed there.

That's when my dad said, "Judah, you have to pace yourself. It's not how you start—it's how you finish."

Today, I wear a bracelet on my left wrist that says, "Better at 70." One of my passions is to be a better follow of Jesus at age seventy than I am now. I want to be a better husband, a better father (and hopefully grandfather), and a better human when I'm seventy.

It's the same principle. Getting off to a good start is fantastic, but what really matters is how we finish. What good is it to be successful, prosperous, and influential now if we get to the end of our lives and find ourselves empty and alone? We should consider what will matter at the end of our lives and make that what matters now.

I think the apostle Paul had a firm grasp on this concept. Toward the end of his life, he told Timothy, his son in the faith:

> *I have fought the good fight, I have finished the race, and I have remained faithful. And now the prize awaits me—the crown of righteousness, which the Lord, the righteous Judge, will give me*

on the day of his return. And the prize is not just for me but for
all who eagerly look forward to his appearing.

(2 Timothy 4:7–8 NLT)

Paul wasn't bragging. He was celebrating. He knew he was nearing the end of his time on Earth, and he had no regrets. Ever since God had knocked Paul off his donkey and introduced him to Jesus, he had lived his life with the end in mind. He had determined his priorities and invested his resources in what really mattered—God, people, love, eternity.

My dad passed away from cancer a few years ago. His illness and passing was the most difficult experience of my life. But as I watched my dad's last days, I got to see firsthand what mattered at the end. We didn't have conversations about the car he drove or the square footage of his house. He didn't tell me how the size of the church he pastored made him happy and satisfied. Instead, we talked about individual people. We talked about kids and grandkids. We reminisced about summer vacations and family Christmases. We talked about how good God is and how real heaven is, and how love makes all the difference in life.

If that's what matters at the end, shouldn't it matter now? Why do we so easily allow things to consume our present that will be irrelevant in our future? I think that often our souls are distracted or overwhelmed simply because we are running unwisely. Either we are burning ourselves out in our hurry to achieve everything all at once—like that third grade race—or we have the wrong goals all along.

As we approach life, let's allow the goal line to shape our race.

Our souls will be healthiest when we are living life with the end in mind.

- What do you want your life to look like at the end?

- Are you currently investing in the things that will matter at the end of your life?

- How does keeping the end in mind help your soul right now?

BATHROOM PERSPECTIVE

A while back, Chelsea was out of town and I was home alone with the kids. It was evening, and I was watching the World Series. That's the only part of the baseball season I watch because there are hundreds or maybe millions of regular season games, and they all last like three hours. I love sports, but that's too much even for me.

It was getting late, so I sent my kids up to get ready for bed. That's when the problems started.

Earlier, I mentioned the instant lethargy and near paralysis that strikes my kids when it's time for their daily routines, which include brushing their teeth. This night was no exception. But I decided I wasn't going to cater to slumped shoulders and ridiculous complaints like, "My arms don't work, so I can't brush my teeth." I was going to take a stand. I'm Dad, after all. That should count for something.

"Go upstairs. You are big boys. Brush your teeth."

I had been watching the World Series for a while when I became aware of odd sounds wafting down the stairs. Sounds like laughing. Chuckling. Moaning. Crying. Splashing. I also realized, to my alarm, these sounds had been going on for several minutes, but my subconscious had been filtering them out. Selective hearing is a parenting survival technique, by the way.

I thought, *Dear Lord, they are just supposed to be brushing their teeth. What is going on?* I went upstairs, opened the bathroom door, and discovered a scene that pushed me over the edge emotionally.

Elliott, who was five at the time, was on the counter. He had a plastic cup in his hands, and he was filling it repeatedly from the faucet and pouring it over his older brother's head as he tried to brush his teeth. Zion wasn't quite sure how to take this, so he alternated between yelling at his brother and laughing. Elliott was semi-hysterical with misguided joy.

As you might have picked up by now, I have a few issues I'm

working through. I can't stand things on the ground, for example. Clutter stresses me out. And if anything gets on my clothes, no matter where I am, I have to change.

So the sight of my five-year-old crouching on a counter, water dripping down the mirror and cascading all over the bathroom, animals lining up two by two to get on the ark—it was too much for me to handle. I lost it. I just started whimpering, "Why?"

I don't even know how the poor kid was supposed to answer that, but I was unrelenting. "Why would you do this? Why?" My whimper went a little higher in pitch and volume.

He shrugged as if to say, "Because I'm five?"

I pretty much started yelling. "Elliott! Why in the world did you do this?" I wasn't thinking—I was just reacting to my son swimming in the bathroom. "Elliott, I said brush your teeth, not build a pool! Why? Why?"

It's always the kid most like you who you are the hardest on. Have you ever noticed that? Inside you're thinking, *Don't be like me. It's a long haul, son. You don't want this life.*

Slowly, Elliott's shoulders dropped. His eyes lost their spark. He let the cup fall, and it bounced to the floor. Still standing on the counter, he mumbled sadly, "Sorry, Dad."

Right about then, the Holy Spirit spoke to me. It wasn't audible—just a feeling in my heart. And it was a lot less angry and demeaning than my tone toward my child. *Son, look what you're doing. Look how much your face and tone affect your child. Elliot isn't the one with the issue here, Judah.*

Not one of my finest fathering moments. I took a deep breath. I apologized. Elliott and I worked through it and hugged.

I explained in a calmer tone what was wrong with his behavior and why water should not be poured on other siblings' heads. We (sort of) mopped up the mess.

But the lesson stayed with me. I had allowed the smallest, pettiest, most ridiculous situation to control my soul. I had permitted things that didn't really matter, such as the state of the bathroom floor, to affect something that mattered far more—my relationship with my kids.

Allowing trivial details and distractions to rule our souls is not limited to parenting. It can happen in any area: our finances, our marriages, our jobs, our health. If we aren't careful, our day-to-day lives can become more reactive than proactive. We can focus more on the problems and frustrations in front of us than on the overall context and trajectory of our lives. Unfortunately, it's all too easy for our souls to become slaves of the petty present and to lose sight of the bigger picture.

The apostle Paul deals with this issue in his letter to the Colossians. He writes:

> Since you have been raised to new life with Christ, set your
> sights on the realities of heaven, where Christ sits in the place
> of honor at God's right hand. Think about the things of heaven,
> not the things of earth. For you died to this life, and your real
> life is hidden with Christ in God.
>
> (Colossians 3:1–3 NLT)

In other words, this life isn't just about this life. Our lives aren't defined by or limited to the here and now. We are "hidden with Christ," which means our lives are wrapped up in his life. Our future is wrapped up in his future.

One of the greatest gifts God gives us as we follow him is the gift of perspective. There is nothing quite like contemplating an infinite God and an eternal heaven to remind us of the transient nature of our current problems. When I consider the lifelong relationship I will have with my kids, a late night flood in the bathroom really isn't a big deal. In the same way, in light of an eternity spent with God, our frustrations and fears fall into their proper perspective.

If you happen to be experiencing some tough moments right now, please don't think I am dismissing what you're going through. The pain and loss are real. But I am inviting you to take a step back from the noise and chaos that want to steal your attention—to pause for a moment and consider how great your God is, how sure your salvation is, and how amazing heaven is going to be.

Your soul is hidden in Jesus and headed for eternity with him. That brings perspective and clarity to any situation. It will help you deal with the fears and uncertainties and disappointments that life brings your way. Your present and your future are secure in Jesus.

- Can you think of a time you allowed petty issues to overwhelm your soul? How did you eventually gain perspective?

- What does it mean to you that your life is "hidden in Jesus"?

- How does contemplating God and heaven help your soul find perspective?

CONCLUSION

Thank you for investing your time and energy in this six-week journey. My hope, prayer, and passion is that this video study and the *How's Your Soul?* book will leave a lasting impact on your soul.

As much as you desire to have a whole, satisfied, and fulfilled soul, God wants it even more. I firmly believe this. God is the creator of the human soul, and he is committed to carrying the work he started in you through to completion. That means you don't have to be the architect of your own growth. You can simply trust him and enjoy the process.

As a matter of fact, the process itself is the most important part of life. What I mean is this: your walk with Jesus is more about relationship with him than anything else. It's not about achieving a higher level of holiness. It's not about not sinning. It's not about what you can do for God. Those things are important, and God wants to help you accomplish them—but ultimately, life is about being with Jesus. It's about enjoying him, learning from him, and following him.

These six weeks are only the beginning. As you learn to lean continually on Jesus, your soul will find greater health and deeper fulfillment than ever before. Even when you go through rocky moments or face uncertain circumstances, your soul will be anchored in Jesus. I truly believe that your best days are still ahead!

LIFE IS _____. How Would You Finish that Sentence?

Judah Smith believes Jesus shows us how to live life to the fullest. In this six-session video study, Judah completes the new sentence again and again, revealing how

- LIFE IS _to be loved and to love_.
- LIFE IS _to trust God in every moment_.
- LIFE IS _to be at peace with God and yourself_.
- LIFE IS _to enjoy God_.

Judah speaks as a friend, welcoming new believers, lifelong followers of Jesus, and even the merely curious. He shows us the love of God that defies human logic and the life that God intends for us to have in the here and now. With excitement and humor, Judah looks at the stories in the Bible from his unique angle and shows how life is all about loving God and loving others.

For more information visit LifeIsBook.tv